Improving English Composition

Edited by
Arno Jewett, Director of the Project, 1962-63
Charles E. Bish, Director of the Project, 1963-

NEA-Dean Langmuir Project on
Improving English Composition

Single copy: cloth, $2.50 (Stock No. 781-10508); paper, $1.50 (Stock
No. 781-10510). Discounts on quantity orders: 2-9 copies, 10 percent;
10 or more copies, 20 percent. All orders not accompanied by payment
will be billed with shipping and handling charges added. Orders
amounting to $2 or less must be accompanied by payment. Order from
and make checks payable to National Education Association, 1201
Sixteenth Street, N.W., Washington, D.C. 20036.

To the memory of

NARCISSA V. STREET

ACKNOWLEDGMENTS

Assistance in the preparation of this publication was provided by the directors of the nine experimental centers during a three-day conference sponsored by the National Education Association and financed, in part, by the Dean Langmuir Foundation. The conference was held in the NEA Building in Washington, D.C., February 24-26, 1964.

While all directors contributed significantly to the plan of the publication, others because of their special knowledge and competencies were asked to contribute to particular areas.

We wish especially to thank Paul B. Diederich, director of research in English, Educational Testing Service, Princeton, New Jersey, for his chapter on grading and for related material appearing in the Appendix; Richard Lander, Shoreline Community College, Seattle, Washington, for the use of his material pertaining to meeting pupil differences through a diversified program; and Joan First, for her contribution as a theme reader. Appreciation is also extended to Jane Power of the NEA Publications Division and to Mary Adams of the Project staff, who assisted admirably with editing and copy preparation.

A special note of gratitude is due the Dean Langmuir Foundation, whose financial support has made this publication and its distribution a reality.

Arno Jewett
Charles E. Bish

Contents

Introduction

The Purpose of This Bulletin

This bulletin is addressed to teachers and administrators who are responsible for the teaching of written composition. The problem has many facets, the most obvious of which is finding adequate teacher time. A tested approach which this publication recommends is the use of theme readers. Other topics explored in this publication are the contribution of linguistics to secondary school composition, the development of a sequential writing program from elementary through high school, the teaching of writing in a deprived cultural environment, relating theme writing to the study of good literature, a defensible philosophy of grading, and new techniques to assess growth in writing.

On the administrative level, there are problems such as schedule making; cooperative arrangements between the English theme reader and teachers of social studies and science; conference time for teacher and student; patterns of evaluation and criticism; selection, payment, and training of theme readers; and articulation between grade levels.

Although none of these is amenable to simple solution, this publication suggests practical approaches requiring only a limited expenditure of funds.

Wide publicity has been given to the inadequate writing ability of high school students. Such deficiencies increase the dropout rate and the number of graduates who fail the College Entrance Examinations. In addition, ineffective writing of college freshmen adds to the dropout rate in college.

New ideas, productive thinking, sound reasons, and appropriate style—none of these can come to fruition unless released through effective written composition. For students to write well requires practice, constructive criticism, and a good deal of individualized help. To do this in an era of mass education requires some experimentation with new procedures and new content plus some risk taking and administrative help. The purpose of this publication is to promote these procedures.

Lawrence G. Derthick
Assistant Executive Secretary
for Educational Services

Highlights of the Project

Arno Jewett
Director of the Project, 1962-63

Charles E. Bish
Director of the Project, 1963-

A tenth-grade boy using an overhead projector to show how he had improved his composition by changing the word order in a few sentences, as suggested by the theme reader—

A teacher, elated because of the help she was receiving from an ex-newspaper writer grading themes, making it possible for every one of 132 pupils to get thorough and constructive criticism of a composition every two weeks—

A round-table discussion of theme readers and English teachers—the subject: How To Grade an English Composition—

These are but three of the many innovations a visitor to any one of the nine NEA-Langmuir English Centers will see as he goes on tour with the project director.

Summer workshops in Baltimore and Cleveland Heights attended by teachers in the program and from nearby systems—

Travel opportunities for teachers—

A lecture on linguistics by an English scholar from a nearby college—

A research plan for the objective measurement of progress worked out in cooperation with state department officials—

A master schedule providing for individual study and conferences—

These comprise highlights of what can be done with a little released time, a few thousand dollars, and the cooperation of a superintendent of schools and his board of education.

With the aid of private funds supplied by the Dean Langmuir Foundation of New York, the National Education Association launched, in 1962, a three-to-five-year project on English composition. The purpose of the project is to improve the quality of composition work in junior and senior high schools by employing what is now accepted as good practice in teaching writing, by utilizing valid research findings in language, and by developing and testing new methods and content.

THE CAUSE FOR CONCERN
ABOUT ENGLISH

During the past few years, businessmen, government officials, college professors, and others who employ or teach the products of the public secondary school have complained about the inability of young people to express themselves clearly and fluently in writing. Several research studies have revealed that poor language ability is one of the factors related positively to pupil dropout rates. High school dropouts or graduates who use slovenly, inexact language in speaking or writing are poor job risks and are, therefore, often found among the unemployed.

The high school graduates now going to college also face formidable tasks requiring composition ability. According to the NCTE report *The National Interest and the Teaching of English* (page 101), an estimated 150,000 students failed their college English test during 1960; almost two thirds of American colleges offer remedial work in English, usually without credit; and the annual cost of teaching remedial English in American colleges approximates 10 million dollars. No one, to our knowledge, has been bold enough to study or even estimate the tremendous financial and social cost of the high dropout rate in higher institutions resulting from failures in freshman composition and other courses where passing grades are largely dependent on one's ability to write term papers and answer essay questions on examinations.

Turning from the student to the teacher and the English program, we find clues to the causes of our failure. The English teacher's work load is often too heavy to permit him to assign many themes and to grade them carefully. Unfortunately, this work load, according to a study reported in the *NEA Research Bulletin* for October 1962, includes eight hours per week which are spent on miscellaneous duties such as monitoring the lunchroom and halls, handling money, keeping records, making reports of all kinds, and performing special administrative assignments. However, these data, which are for secondary school teachers in general, do not reflect all the extra hours the English teacher spends chaperoning student parties, acting as a penny-ante banker, and engaging in other duties that could be performed by parents, clerks, or part-time employees.[1] For example, there is no reason why a retired teacher could not be employed for part-time duty to manage study halls at an hourly rate substantially lower than that paid teachers. Then teachers would have time to become scholarly in their academic fields, to keep abreast of new research and literature, and to teach individuals and small groups that need special attention. When one realizes the effect of these nonteaching duties, one can appreciate why the delegates at the NEA convention in Denver set "Time To Teach" second on their list of seven professional priorities for 1962-65.

The rationale for the English Composition Project is also based on the need to economize on time in the English program, to individualize instruction, to develop sequential language programs from elementary school into college, to make students independent, self-reliant writers, to introduce worthwhile content into the composition sequence, to experiment with new approaches, and to translate research findings into classroom practices. Studies have proved that there is a tremendous amount of unnecessary repetition in the English curriculum, especially for average and above-average students. Many students are taught to write letters of application in every grade of the secondary school. One boy reported that he had written his autobiography 13 times during a six-year period.

Much time could be saved in English classes if, instead of drilling students annually on how to address a letter to a senator or judge, or how to punctuate quotations within quotations, or how to hyphenate compound words, teachers showed pupils where and how to find this type of information whenever they had need for it. Instead, teachers persist in their futile struggle against the psychological laws of disuse and forgetting as they

---

[1] This extra work may be one cause of the severe shortage of English teachers. The actual supply of new English teachers in 1963 was only 65 percent of the number employed in 1964. (See the *NEA Research Bulletin* for December 1964, page 122.)

try year after year to drill linguistic trivia and outdated language rules into the minds of their students.

And, too, some schools, while recognizing individual differences in words, ignore them in practice. Although differences in pupil achievement are readily observable in language and composition and are considered in dealing with both functional illiterates and gifted, quite frequently the gifted pupil is asked to do twice as many of the same simple exercises as the slow pupil. Such busywork assignments lead to an inordinate waste of time for the good student and often to an ingrained dislike for English.

But the total problem involves more than "time to teach" and "lack of communication between teachers" or providing a good sequential curriculum. As important as these are, scholarship among those "assigned to English classes" and the need for additional preparation are, for the country as a whole, an equally serious problem.

To quote from the survey conducted by the Committee on the National Interest of the National Council of Teachers of English, only half of the high school English teachers earned college majors in English. One third of the rest did not have majors in a related field such as speech or journalism.

The average English teacher has taught for nine years but during the past decade 30 percent have taken no course work in English; 25 percent, no course work in education.

Although almost 90 percent said they wanted to study intermediate or advanced composition, the average secondary teacher has completed less than one semester hour in composition or linguistics since starting to teach.

Evaluating themselves, 86 percent of the secondary school teachers did not feel well prepared to teach reading; more than 60 percent felt ill prepared to teach composition or speech; and more than 40 percent felt inadequate to teach literature and language.

Fewer than 20 percent of the elementary teachers have majors in English. Although English comprises 24 percent of the elementary program, courses in English and the teaching of English total less than 8 percent of their course work.

However, a good deal of help is on the way: the English program of the U.S. Office of Education is bringing together English teachers to develop curriculum and teaching methods from kindergarten to post high school levels. The expanded NDEA Bill S-3060, which includes institutes for teacher in-service education for English for the first time, and the Cooperative Research Program of the U.S. Office of Education, which provides grants through universities and state departments of education for the purpose of curriculum improvement and experimental work in English, will soon begin to have a significant impact upon instruction from kindergarten through grade 12.

THE RATIONALE

Here then is the thinking behind the Project. Grants were made in 1962 to five school districts and in 1963 to four additional school districts.[2] In each school system it was understood that the life of the grants would be from three to five years and that, insofar as possible, the several boards of education would assume an increasingly large share of the cost of the Project each year so that at the conclusion of the period of annual grants each program might become an integral and accepted part of the regular school program.

The administration in each school agreed to relieve participating English teachers of some nonprofessional duties such as study hall supervision, bus duty, ticket selling, and clerical work, as well as to reduce each teacher's class load to between 120 and 150 students. To lighten the teacher's paper work, the administration in each center has employed 6 to 10 theme readers to read and correct approximately three quarters of the themes written in representative English classes. Rates for theme readers vary from $1.75 to $2.50 per hour. Each English teacher involved in the program is assigned one theme reader and an alternate. The English teacher skims all themes and corrects carefully at least a fourth of those written for each assignment. By reading papers written by a different quarter of the class during a cycle of four assignments, the teacher is able to keep informed of each pupil's progress and to compare his grading with that of the theme reader. Theme readers also read long compositions or research papers that pupils write in science, history, and other courses after the science or history teacher has read and graded them for content. In this way the same standards for pupil composition work are being followed in all classes, for the student is given an English grade for all the major papers he writes in school.

Most of the pupils' themes are written in class during a one- or two-period session when the English teacher is available to provide individualized help to pupils who need it the most. English classes that meet for a double period are scheduled once

---

2 See page 112 for the distribution and location of the experimental centers.

every other week on a back-to-back basis with history or some other required subject. During the week when a double period is scheduled, English class is omitted one day so that students can attend history or the other subject for two periods. Classrooms have been equipped with language handbooks, indexes to grammar and usage, paperback thesauri, dictionaries, and other reference books found in a newspaper or publishing office. In some centers, the senior high school teachers are experimenting with handbooks used in college composition courses in which their students expect to be enrolled within a year or two. This is an attempt to bridge the language and composition chasm between the senior year of high school and the first year of college.

Since the English teacher has been freed of at least one study hall and various clerical duties, he has time to hold individual conferences with students during their free periods or regular class time when they are engaged in supervised study. During these conferences, teacher and student examine the themes which the student has already written and revised during the school year. Usually a 10-minute conference to note language deficiencies and progress is held monthly. Themes written by each student are placed in a manila folder and filed in a classroom cabinet where they are available at all times for use by the theme reader and teacher. Some teachers engaged in the Project forward each pupil's folder of themes and other papers at the end of the academic year to the principal's office, which in turn transmits the themes to the pupil's next English teacher for his use in planning the coming year's language and composition program. Under consideration is a plan whereby these English teachers will be paid to work a week analyzing pupils' themes before the school year begins. This type of diagnosis will, we believe, give the teacher a much more accurate reflection of each pupil's weaknesses than the administration of a diagnostic test in language which contains contrived sentences replete with blanks by a test-maker, who may not have kept informed on matters of linguistic change.

Another effort to economize on time is being made in the area of curriculum. English teachers in composition centers have surveyed the writing assignments given in the elementary and secondary schools of their district and have eliminated much needless duplication of effort. Also, they are preparing different types of writing sequences for slow, average, and superior students in accord with their anticipated needs. Scope and sequence charts which outline the type and length of composition assignments from elementary school through high school are making it possible for teachers to know what is being taught at all levels.

Better use of instructional time is also being achieved by introducing writing assignments that deal with significant ideas in language and literature. Instead of writing on topics like "Why Ma Fights with Pa," "My Pet Peeve," and "My Most Embarrassing Moment," students study articles about their language: its history, syntax, and semantics; levels of usage; dialects; metaphor; the power of language; dictionaries and their use. Then students compose themes on topics relevant to the content of the articles studied. Thus, they learn about their language and think and write about it. They also write about significant ideas or major characters in great pieces of literature that they read. They may discuss the author's theme, the motives of characters, the conflict and its resolution, or the appropriateness of diction and style. In doing these assignments, students are expected to exercise their critical judgment and to improve their literary taste and discrimination. Theme readers, of course, also read the teacher's assignments in language and literature so that they can intelligently evaluate the content of students' compositions.

As has been mentioned, theme readers are being employed by each of the nine school districts. They were carefully selected from a large number of outstanding applicants possessing college degrees and a major in English. Here is what Leonard Freyman, of the Cleveland Heights City School District, wrote about his applicants: "Of the approximately 100 letters received, many are from Phi Beta Kappa, summa and magna cum laude graduates with a Master's degree in English. Many have had professional writing, publishing and editing experience." There seems to be no shortage of qualified potential theme readers in the urban sections of America. However, before candidates were employed, they were required to take a test on conventional usage, grammar, and rhetoric; to evaluate pupil themes; and to write an impromptu theme of several hundred words. An important requirement was that theme readers be in a position to read and return themes promptly. After the most promising applicants were screened from the total number, English teachers met socially with those they thought they wanted to work with and then made their choices.

After being selected, theme readers were oriented through a workshop aimed at acquainting them with (a) the school organization, (b) their responsibilities, (c) the composition program and requirements in the city's elementary and secondary schools, (d) standards desired at each grade level, (e) ways to grade and correct themes to improve student writing, and (f) handbooks and language books used by local English teachers.

During the first two or three months, English teachers worked closely with their theme readers in order to ensure that papers were carefully corrected and graded in accordance with the teachers' standards. As a result, some teachers found that they were working longer hours than they normally did; however, as their confidence in the theme reader increased, the teachers' work load was lightened appreciably.

Parents of students enrolled in classes served by theme readers seem to be extremely pleased with the results thus far, especially with the detailed, constructive comments that are made on pupils' compositions. Theme readers have said that they enjoy their work. Teachers and their pupils have also commented favorably about the total composition program. And teachers of courses other than English have stated that their students' written work is being more carefully prepared than it was in previous years. Here, for example, is a science teacher's reaction:

> This is my first experience in cooperating with the English Department and their current writing laboratory program.
> I have observed that my biology students involved in this program were more conscientious in their efforts to improve their writing techniques. They were told that their papers were to be read by a reader as well as myself. One grade was to go for grammar, mechanics, etc. and the other for biology. This, I think, had its effect (which was good!) on all concerned.
> I am very much impressed with the quality of these papers as compared with the papers of a similar assignment last year.

During the present academic year 1964-65 each center is emphasizing particular phases of its program through expanded activities. Among these are—

1. A determination of whether instruction in both oral English and written composition produces more improvement than intensive instruction in written composition alone in the areas of usage, mechanics, and clarity of expression. The experiment is being carried on with both eighth- and eleventh-grade pupils of average ability.

2. Development of sequential programs from kindergarten through senior high school.

3. Demonstration classes for teachers and theme readers.

4. An attempt to test the efficiency of conventional drills on errors in themes and theme revision.

5. A comparison of the impact upon improvement in written composition of SRA materials used with an overhead projector and the same materials used through conventional methods.

6. An exploration of the effect upon progress in composition writing when theme readers are used with combination English-social studies classes and with classes of only English.

Other Supporting Activities—1964

In February a three-day Conference of the Center Directors was held at the National Education Association Headquarters Building, 1201 Sixteenth Street, N.W., in Washington, for the purpose of sharing experiences, reporting problems and progress, and planning this publication. Arno Jewett served as general consultant for the Conference. Special guests included Paul B. Diederich, director of research in English, Educational Testing Service; Arthur W. Brown, assistant director, Advanced Placement Program, College Entrance Examination Board; Virgil Walker, U.S. Office of Education; and Robert C. Snider, assistant executive secretary, Division of Audiovisual Instruction, National Education Association.

Project personnel enjoyed two opportunities to participate in the NEA convention in Seattle in 1964. On the evening of July 1 theme readers from Greensboro, North Carolina; Lansing, Michigan; Richmond, Virginia; Seattle, Washington; and Wichita, Kansas, presented a round-table discussion with Charles E. Bish as moderator at the educational studios of the University of Washington. Again, on the afternoon of July 2, the same theme readers participated in a panel discussion program with Helen F. Olson, director, English Language Arts, and director of the Project in Seattle, as chairman.

The Baltimore, Wichita, and Greensboro summer workshops were particularly ambitious. Seattle and Cleveland Heights developed curriculum materials which they shared with all other Project centers. Richmond, Baltimore, Cleveland Heights, and Lake Charles plan to carry on extensive research programs to test the results they are getting.

It is not possible to mention all the creative ideas being tried out in the nine composition centers or all the research which is being planned. Every center is developing and experimenting with old and new approaches.

In summary, the Project in each demonstration center aims to—

1. Give the English teacher more time to concentrate on the teaching of writing by freeing him of many nonprofessional duties and by giving him help in the form of qualified theme readers.

2. Train students to become independent and self-reliant writers by having them do composition work during class hours in a room well equipped with reference aids like those in an editorial office.

3. Provide a sequential language and composition program from elementary school into college.

4. Give each student instructional help on a personal basis through individual conferences with the teacher.

5. Experiment with new approaches to teaching writing and to introducing linguistic and literary content into the composition program.

6. Provide regional demonstration centers for English teachers and supervisors to visit so they can observe promising patterns of instruction.

Data now being assembled will be used to determine—

1. The relative merits of student writing assignments completed in and out of the classroom.

2. The effectiveness of teacher-pupil conferences based on the student's writing.

3. The most successful ways to utilize theme readers.

4. The nature of college composition programs.

5. The value of linguistic approaches in teaching composition.

Thus far, teachers, pupils, parents, theme readers, and principals seem pleased with their programs. Actually, the programs can be adopted or adapted by any school system, with only a small outlay for theme readers and reference books.

Many features of the program that are good are not original, and many parts that are experimental may prove to have little value. But notwithstanding the inherent risks, we are seeking a better way to teach students to write.

2

Initiating a Program

Nancy Millett
English Teacher and Director of the Project
Wichita Public Schools

The problems of initiating a program in composition can
be formidable, but dissatisfied people determined to make a difference can make a difference that matters. Let us suppose the
worst. Let us suppose that the existing program in composition
is a program in name only, that there is no consistently developed sequence from grades 7 to 12 or even from grades 10 to 12;
or that where a sequence has been developed, it is sketchily outlined, weakly implemented, or adhered to in only one school in a
multischool system. Let us suppose further that teachers feel
inadequately trained to teach composition, that they have no
confidence in further exposure to the college departments of
English and education that failed to train them to teach composition in the first place, and that they feel heavily burdened
by student load and extracurricular duties—because in truth
they are. Finally, let us suppose that it is harder this year than
it was last year to find funds for new programs and that no
procedure has been established to evaluate a program that might
be initiated. Without exaggeration, these are the problems con-
fronting many boards of education, administrators, and teachers
throughout the country.

Despite vigorous efforts by many teachers and despite the employment of some theme readers since 1959 to assist secondary teachers of English, problems such as these could be found in Wichita, Kansas, in June of 1963.[1] Within one year every one of these problems has been cut down to size.

Anyone can be the individual who begins to make the difference. An administrator or a member of the board of education will probably think of money first, personnel second, and a program third. A department chairman or a teacher will probably have a hunch about a program, need some time, and hope for money. None of these individuals is likely to worry about establishing procedures to evaluate a program until it is too late. Whatever one's position, and whatever his prejudices, the fact is that all of these problems must be confronted if anything is to be done. Where one starts does not matter. Starting does matter.

For practical purposes, I suggest that those determined to make a difference begin with the problem of outlining a program. Unless planning is done, overcoming the other problems of time, training, money, and evaluation is meaningless. Agreement upon the bare outlines of a program for one school at one grade level, or preferably in two adjoining grades, is enough to build upon. Any diversity resulting from teachers in a number of schools working out different programs should be welcomed as a sign of experimentation and ultimate strength rather than regarded as a sign of uncertainty.

Once the first step has been taken, productive work can begin in each of six areas. Since all 13 teachers who participated in the first year of the NEA Project in English Composition in Wichita have said that they wish to participate again next year, and since 11 of these 13 teachers have said that their ability to teach composition has improved "a great deal" as a result of the Project, I feel confident in suggesting their ideas and procedures to others.

1. *The program.* Assuming that each English teacher in grades 10 and 11 has five classes of 30 students each and that he grades six papers an hour six and a quarter hours a week for 36 weeks (or seven and a half hours a week for 30 weeks), he can grade about nine papers a year for each student—a minimum requirement from students in return for a maximum effort from teachers. Structuring this work is essential.

---

[1] The Wichita Public Schools include six senior high schools, grades 10 to 12, and fourteen junior high schools, grades 7 to 9.

Teachers should agree on a program that is sequential and that provides for implementation of each step in the sequence by means of careful preparation for each writing assignment. Each assignment should be based on the major points that have been presented, and provisions should be made for careful grading followed by thorough revision of at least half of the papers. To omit or to slight any of these minimum requirements is to work counter to what is known about the teaching and learning of composition.[2]

At Wichita High School East, teachers agreed to follow a sequential program in grades 10 and 11 based upon various methods of paragraph development. In grade 10, development by reasons, by examples, by comparison-contrast, and by a combination of these methods was stressed, with special attention to transitions or connectors relevant to each method. In grade 11, following a review of these methods, development by definition of a concrete term and definition of an abstract term, note-taking, précis writing, and the writing of research papers were taught. The sequence for both grades also specified a progression from shorter to longer papers and from experiential to literary subjects.

2. *Time.* In order to provide teachers with time to plan a program and to grade the papers, the administration agreed to release participating teachers from all extracurricular assignments. Teachers from other departments, who often go home happily unencumbered by papers, assumed these duties.

Depending upon the number of teachers and classes to be involved in the program, released time should also be given a director—a curriculum coordinator, a department chairman, or a classroom teacher. Needless to say, this one person should be well trained to teach composition, should expect to work *at least* two to four hours every day on the program, and should have easy access to secretarial help at least two hours a day. Release from two classes is absolutely essential if a classroom teacher is expected to give meaningful direction.

3. *Training personnel.* To counteract teachers' feelings of inadequacy through in-service training is difficult. The simplest, quickest, least expensive, and most effective method I know of

---

[2] See Braddock, Richard; Lloyd-Jones, Richard; and Schoer, Lowell. *Research in Written Composition.* Champaign, Ill.: National Council of Teachers of English, 1963. Chapter 3, "The State of Knowledge About Composition," pp. 29-53.

training teachers and students at the same time is to set up a series of demonstrations. To do this, teachers agree on a schedule for presenting the six or seven basic steps in the composition sequence, usually at monthly intervals. Having specified the basic idea for each step, either the director or another teacher working with the director prepares a demonstration lesson to present to all students on the same day.

In each demonstration, the instructor focuses attention on one seminal idea. For example, he explains why a method of paragraph development is worth mastering, shows students how to organize and develop relevant support around a single controlling idea, and asks students to work through a sample problem with him. If time permits and an overhead projector is available, the demonstrator can also show students a sample paper previously written by a student on that same problem and invite discussion about what could be done to improve the paper. If these demonstrations are held at least four out of the six periods in the day, every English teacher in the school, whether or not his classes are part of the program, has an opportunity to see the demonstration—and to see it *as it works in the classroom,* not in a vacuum. (If demonstrations cannot be held in a room large enough to accommodate two—but no more than two— classes meeting at the same time, the demonstrator can move from room to room throughout the day.)

On the day following each demonstration, a writing assignment can be distributed to each class. Designed by the demonstrator to emphasize and illustrate the main points of the demonstration, each writing assignment should give detailed instructions about how to develop one of several possible subjects from which the student can choose to show his understanding of the method being studied. (About 80 percent of 392 students in grade 10 and about 70 percent of 389 students in grade 11 reported that having a choice of subject helped them to write a better paper.)

4. *Workshop training*. To strengthen the training of teachers and to build a stronger program for students, the director should make provisions early in the year for a summer workshop. This workshop need be only one week in length, with teachers meeting six hours a day under the direction of an instructor, preferably one who is familiar with the specific interests and needs of the local group. The instructor might well follow the program designed at the Wichita State University in June of 1964. In this workshop, teachers were shown other sequential

programs developed in this country. They were then provided with an outline for analyzing these courses of study before hearing reports on how they compared with one another and with the local program. Following this analysis, the instructor illustrated a step in a sequence by presenting a sample demonstration and a writing assignment based upon it, plus samples of students' writing in response to the assignment. Groups of teachers were then ready to revise their own sequences or to draw up the outlines for new ones, accompanied by individually prepared plans for a demonstration and a writing assignment to implement one step in the sequence. A third unit, dealing with problems of revision and of evaluation, concluded the Wichita workshop, which 100 percent of the teachers said was the most meaningful training they had ever had in how to teach composition.

5. *Evaluation.* Once a program is clearly outlined and teachers have identified specific questions they wish to study (for example, the effect of revising papers compared to the effect of doing drill work on errors made in papers), the director should seek the advice of an experienced statistician about how to set up an experiment and to measure its results. Failure to do this beforehand is fatal to any study. If the local school system cannot provide this service, the nearest university can and usually will help.

6. *Money.* At the very least, money to initiate a program must be available to release one teacher from two classes, provide a substitute for the demonstrator on each of seven demonstration days in grades 10 and 11, secure the services of a part-time secretary, buy enough reams of paper to mimeograph monthly writing assignments following each demonstration, and pay the workshop instructor—unless a nearby university is willing to carry this last cost. Assuming that a $6,000-a-year teacher is to be released from two classes, that substitutes cost $25 a day, that a clerk-typist will work 300 hours during the year for $1.25 an hour, that $100 will buy ample mimeograph supplies, and that $500 will be paid to the workshop instructor, the total cost of initiating a program in composition would be approximately $3,725, or less than the cost of one part-time teacher. Better, if an additional $2,000 to $3,000 were disbursed at $2 an hour to theme readers who could evaluate the organization and mechanics of 8 to 10 papers an hour, students could write more frequently, and the program would still cost no more than the salary of one teacher earning $6,000 a year. In return, dozens of teachers and thousands of students could benefit. A strong

composition program would replace a weak one, teachers would be more fully equipped to meet their professional obligations and would be far happier attempting to do so, and taxpayers would know that they were supporting work that adds to the state of knowledge about the teaching and learning of composition.

One person can start to make this difference.

3

The Six-Year Seattle Program

Helen F. Olson
Director, English Language Arts
Seattle Public Schools

The Administrative, Instructional, and Curriculum Divisions of the Seattle Public Schools—and the English Language Arts Department in particular—welcomed the opportunity to become one of the centers of NEA Project Composition, thus benefiting from a grant made possible by the Dean Langmuir Foundation. The staff of the Seattle Public Schools is continuously searching out ways of improving teaching and learning, constantly endeavoring to approach more nearly the goal of enabling each student to reach his potential in skills, understandings, and appreciations. One important competence is ability in written composition; and the NEA grant offers assistance in this area.

THE IMPORTANCE OF WRITTEN COMPOSITION

Written composition is important to persons at all ages and in all walks of life. Competence in written composition is important in school and college, on the job, and in social and civic life.

The person who writes fluently and clearly has an asset that will serve him well and that increases in value with added experience.

Ability in written composition, more than ability in any other aspect of language, is the product of the English classroom. A person gains experience in reading, in listening, and in speaking from many sources outside the English classroom and indeed outside the school; but guidance in writing, for most students, is largely confined to the classroom—and to the English classroom most specifically. Therefore teaching of written composition deserves special consideration.

Another reason for the importance of written composition is that writing, if properly taught, can be the focus of all English language arts teaching and can make this a unified, spiraling learning experience for students, rather than a somewhat amorphous, and to that extent meaningless, study of many unrelated skills. The Seattle course of study, *Guideposts to the English Language Arts, Kindergarten Through Grade Twelve,* has been developed to focus on written composition. The work of each grade level, kindergarten through grade 12, is organized to develop through a spiraling sequence what is in Seattle called *the composition process.* Each composition process includes five steps which, together, cover all aspects of the English language arts course:

1. Reading, thinking, and discussing
2. Planning the writing
3. Writing
4. Proofreading, sharing, revising, rewriting, filing for future reference
5. Teaching and learning of language skills.

Such a composition process lends itself to an infinite number of variations in approach, content, kinds of oral and written presentations, and length of time to be needed for each application of the process. The average time needed is two weeks. Several applications of the composition process, grouped about a central theme, constitute a teaching unit or division. Several teaching units constitute a year's course. And each year's work in the English language arts course builds upon the skills, knowledge, and understandings gained during the previous years. Thus, in Seattle, the entire sequence of English language arts work, kindergarten through grade 12, focuses upon written composition and incorporates the composition process.

SEATTLE CENTER OF NEA "PROJECT COMPOSITION"

Explanation of Organization

The organization of the Seattle center of NEA Project Composition is as follows: seven grade levels are covered—grades 6 through 12; teachers participating include five grade 6 teachers, twelve grade 7 to 9 teachers, and seven grade 10 to 12 teachers; four schools are included—two elementary schools, one junior high school, and one senior high school; fourteen lay readers have been hired to read themes—one for each elementary school, six for the junior high school, and six for the senior high school.

Several questions have been raised concerning this organization. For instance, *how was it determined?* First, the director of English language arts conferred with the assistant superintendent for curriculum. Then a small group consisting of these two and the deputy superintendent, the assistant superintendent for secondary schools, and the assistant superintendent for elementary schools met at two sessions to decide the organization likely to be most helpful for the participants and for the system as a whole.

Why were grades 6 to 12 selected for this experimental work? The selection is in accordance with the interest of Seattle schools in articulation from grade level to grade level, especially articulation between the elementary school and the junior high school and between the junior high school and the senior high school. Because of pressure of other subjects and many demands upon the elementary school teacher—also because the elementary school teacher has seldom had more than a college freshman course in composition—written composition is sometimes inadequately taught in the elementary school, particularly in the intermediate grades (4-6). As a result the gap may be too great between what is taught in grade 6 and what is expected in grade 7.

Guidelines have been developed which suggest steps indicating how improved articulation may be accomplished at each of the several grade levels. Each teacher is provided with the entire sequence in the publication *Guideposts to the English Language Arts*. This includes four sets of expected attainments for the reasonably well-prepared pupil: one at the end of grade 3, one at the end of grade 6, one at the end of grade 9, and one at the end of grade 12.

Some progress has been made, too, toward clearer understanding and closer agreement concerning the criteria to be used
in evaluating written work, through city-wide theme tests at
grades 9 and 11 and some grouped theme testing of grade 6
pupils in several schools. All theme tests are graded by groups
of teachers who work with the English Language Arts Department in determining the criteria and then discuss the criteria
in terms of the papers being corrected and the reports to be
made to the other classroom teachers. It seemed that papers
from the lower grades might be too short to justify the cost of
theme readers; therefore it was decided to begin with grade 6.
Another reason for including grade 6 is that the aim is to keep
a record of the growth in ability of the students in written composition through their public school years and, to the extent
possible, into college.

*How many teachers, students, and theme readers are now
in the Project?* It was decided that, since one theme reader could
probably serve at least two elementary teachers, 16 teachers
and 14 theme readers would be included. Some teachers do not
have all five classes at the same grade level. Therefore, two or
more teachers, each having from one to three classes in the
Project, work with the same theme reader. There are 24 teachers, 2 department heads, and about 2,300 students in Project
Composition.

Steps for the Project
During the First Year

The first step, after the initial planning had been done, was
to consult principals and department heads and, when these had
expressed the desire to participate in Project Composition, to
select teachers to be included—the choices of these to be largely
at the discretion of the principals and department heads—and
to hold some initial meetings and conferences concerning the
opportunities and limitations of the Project, specific aims for
Seattle, and ways of initiating the Project and carrying it forward. All persons consulted wished to include grade 6, since
staff members in Seattle are aware of the value of sequence in
achieving and maintaining steady growth in skills and understandings for all students.

The second step was to hire theme readers. The Personnel
Division inserted notices in local papers and had short announce-
ments read over the radio and television. As a result, more than

one hundred persons applied during the two-week period allowed for submitting applications. Eighty-five completed the filling out of applications and appeared for the two-and-a-half-hour test the following week. As a result of ratings in the three-part test, consisting of an English essentials test, interlinear correcting of a theme, and writing of a theme, 14 theme readers were selected. We now have a considerable listing of very able persons who can be called upon when and if we need additional readers. The rate of payment decided upon for theme readers is $2.50 an hour for conferences, 20¢ for a grade 6 or grade 7 theme, 25¢ for a grade 8 or grade 9 theme, and 35¢ for a grade 10, 11, or 12 theme.

The third step was an orientation day for the theme readers and the participating classroom teachers. Reference books, criteria for grading, handling of papers, and other such matters were discussed fully, and agreements were reached. Also, through an informal arrangement, theme readers and classroom teachers were paired and then had a chance to talk together and to become acquainted. This orientation day extended from 8:30 A.M. to 3:00 P.M. Substitutes for the teachers and $2.50 an hour for the theme readers (who were brought into the afternoon program only) were paid from the special fund.

The fourth step is the one which we are taking currently. Consultations are being held with participating teachers and with theme readers. The principals are explaining the Project to other members of the school staff. Procedures are being tried out for collecting and returning papers. The criteria for paper correcting set up during the orientation day are being tried out. Care is taken to see that the theme readers have the necessary reference materials and that a copy of the assignment, together with a list of criteria set up by teacher and class for that particular writing lesson, accompany each set of papers given to the theme reader for correcting. The Business Division has cooperated with the English Language Arts Department by setting up a method for handling the special fund and disbursing the money.

During the spring semester, a series of demonstrations will enable participants to share their experience and thinking with others. There will be eight demonstrations, one for each grade level, grades 7 through 12, and two for grade 6, because two elementary schools are included. Another reason for planning two grade 6 demonstrations is that Seattle staff members are particularly interested in what happens in the grade 6 classrooms. Persons invited to the spring demonstrations will include not only members of the Seattle staff but also interested persons from other school systems. During this beginning series of demonstrations, effort will be made to give first consideration to curriculum leaders and other key persons in our own and neighboring communities who may wish to attend.

Plan for Evaluating the Project

The value of any project such as NEA Project Composition is appropriately measured only by its influence on students. Detailed objective evaluation will be handled through the Research Division. However, several measures are being taken which will facilitate any research and/or evaluation to be undertaken later.

A follow-up of these 2,300 students is being planned. There will be an attempt to keep the students now in the Project in classes of participating teachers until the students complete high school. This means careful records and special assignments of students over the years.

The English Language Arts Department has now on file a theme written at the beginning of the year by each student. These themes will be retained for reference and can, when compared with themes written at future periods, be one means of evaluating pupil progress.

Meeting Pupil Differences

Through a Diversified Composition Program

Richard Lander
Former Chairman, Shoreline High School English Department
*Seattle Public Schools**

The following article is based on the curriculum in composition and language of the Shoreline High School, Seattle, Washington, developed by Richard Lander, chairman of the English Department, and his staff.

A pitfall of many high school composition programs is that a single standard of performance and a single type of learning activity are set for all pupils within the same class. Many a teacher's struggles reflect the two- or three-pronged dilemma, "What is a good composition for students of differing abilities and interests at different levels of maturity?" Themes will differ in length, vocabulary or diction, sentence variety, use of figura-

* Mr. Lander was formerly chairman of the English Department, Shoreline High School; presently he is chairman of the Humanities Division, Shoreline Community College, and chairman of the NCTE Committee on High School-College Articulation. Among offices currently held by Mr. Lander are those of member, CEEB Planning Institute; member, National Council for Accreditation of Teacher Education; chairman, Curriculum Commission, Washington State Council of Teachers of English; and member, NCTE Committee on Teacher Preparation and Certification.

tive language, style, and content or treatment of the subject. Topics for themes also should vary, from grade to grade.

More and more high schools are becoming aware of the need to accommodate to the diversified needs, abilities, and interests of their pupils. Teachers of English from grades 7 through 12 are starting to formulate progressively mature requirements for each grade level. In some cases, they are also following the recommended practice of selecting sample themes representing superior, average, and unsatisfactory achievement for each grade. These samples generally represent each important type of writing activity on which course time is spent: social letters, business letters, exposition, description, reports, and criticism.

Thus, when students in, for example, grade 11 are writing book reviews, they may be handed mimeographed examples of superior, average, and unsatisfactory literary reviews prepared by students (names eliminated) in previous years. These are carefully studied in class and evaluated by teacher and students, using a composition rating scale which English teachers at each high school level have jointly agreed upon and distributed in their classes. Hence, students become aware of the differences among superior, average, and inferior compositions.

Some high schools are employing diversified programs in teaching English and composition. A few maintain as many as four distinct curriculums, developed according to abilities, levels of achievement, and needs or levels of aspiration of the students. These programs also take into account students' increasing maturity and presumed mastery as they progress from grade to grade or year to year.

Shoreline's program for teaching English is in large measure directed toward three objectives:

To develop the student's ability to communicate in well-organized, literate speech and writing.
To develop the student's ability to understand and to appreciate the literature of our culture.
To help the student understand the history and structure of the language.

Although content of the four courses, even at the same grade level, varies considerably, the actual work load at each level is about the same. It is the emphasis and depth of study, not generally the amount of time consumed by the course participants, that differentiates one level of achievement from another. The four courses are variously identified; one suggested classification is *honors, intensive, regular,* and *basic.* Each course encompasses writing, speaking, language, and either reading or literature. The eleventh-grade basic program also embraces listening for such purposes as following directions, judging television, radio, and movie performances, etc. Aside from the differentiation of content, assignments, and goals for students of varying ability, the distinctive features of the program are the emphasis on logical thinking in the composition work of superior students and the use of literature as a source of ideas for much of the writing.

HONORS PROGRAM

To get an idea of sequence used, consider first the *honors* program, which might enroll, in a comprehensive secondary school, about 3 percent of the class. To enter this program from the junior high school, the pupil should generally have a minimum IQ of about 120 (as much as a 10-point variation can be justified when all facts are considered) ; he should have a record of achievement above grade level in reading and language as measured by standard tests and by junior high school grades; he should have achieved a verbal aptitude score which places him in the upper 5 percent of his class ; he must be recommended by teachers and counselor and must produce a successful entrance essay; his parents should consent to his placement; and the student must be willing to enter a challenging program. To remain in the course, the student must continue to perform at the honors level.

The course composition content at this level in grade 10 includes inductively and deductively developed descriptive and expository paragraphs; short expository themes based chiefly on literature; précis, paraphrase, and essay tests; concentration on precise wording and on logical organization. A theme or paper is written about every seven class days.

In the eleventh grade, the student enrolled in the honors program prepares short expository themes of definition, comparison and contrast, and analysis. Subject matter is derived from literature and from the humane concepts underlying developments in the social studies area. Students write short source-based papers and, as in the tenth grade, précis, paraphrase, and essay tests. During this year, the concentration is on economical development of thesis, support of generalization, logical transition, and development of fluency by frequent in-class papers. A theme is required about every ten class days.

Concentration on expository, analytical writing and argument on literary subjects takes place in the senior year. The students prepare short source-based papers using standard footnote and bibliographic forms. A theme is assigned about every seven class days. A good quantity gauge is approximately 5,000 words a semester. To develop writing fluency, the teacher may well require that every third theme be written in class. Emphasis is also given to the essay test, paraphrase, and précis and to note-taking on lecture materials.

Language studies in the honors program at the tenth-grade level include an introduction to semantics, connotation and denotation, context as determinant of meaning, and levels of language appropriate for various audiences. Language structure and usage are taught in relation to writing needs. There is emphasis on vocabulary and spelling.

In the junior-year honors course, the history of American English is frequently emphasized along with levels of usage and the ladder of abstraction. Conventional usage and spelling are strengthened; students come to see the structure of language as related to writing and are trained in precise and effective use of words.

History of the English language and introduction to structural linguistics might well be taught in the senior year, through the use of Charlton Laird's *Miracle of Language*. There is individual concentration on errors of usage as these appear in writing and insistence on improvement in mechanical matters.

INTENSIVE PROGRAM

The second level of difficulty in the English curriculum is known as the *intensive* course. It, like the honors track, is a college-preparatory curriculum. Following favorable counselor, teacher, and parent recommendation, it may be elected by students requiring a high-level college-preparatory course and is so chosen by at least 40 to 60 percent of secondary school pupils in the average and above comprehensive high school. In order to remain in the group, the student must be able to perform at the intensive level.

Tenth-grade writing initially concentrates on deductively developed descriptive and expository paragraphs, with subjects drawn primarily (not exclusively) from literature. As the students mature, they progress to three- or four-paragraph papers. Emphasis is on good word choice, adequate statement of thesis, sufficient supporting detail, and transition. The précis, paraphrase, and essay tests are used. It is suggested that a paper be assigned about every ten days.

The junior-year intensive writing program is concentrated on expository themes utilizing both inductively and deductively developed paragraphs on subjects from both literature and the humane content of history. Additional work is done on précis of library sources and on paraphrase. Essay tests are used. Short (400-word) source-based papers are assigned. One theme is assigned every 10 class days, including ten or twelve 300- to 400-word papers a semester, as well as three to five somewhat longer class papers. Elementary logic is introduced.

Senior-year written work at the intensive level emphasizes expository themes, mainly on humanistic and literary subjects. Study is made of the anatomy of research papers, and there are short, practice source-based papers on literary or background subjects. Stress is placed on logic, especially its formal uses in writing. One theme is assigned each 10 class days, with the expectation of ten to twelve 400-word papers a semester, including three to five impromptu class papers (a library paper can replace two short papers). Précis, paraphrase, and essay test work are continued, and the class is expected to take notes on lecture material.

Intensive-level language work for the tenth grade involves study of language levels appropriate to the audience, the writer, and the material. Usage and language structures as related to speech and writing are studied, as are vocabulary and spelling. Concreteness in language is emphasized.

The eleventh-grade intensive course includes the history of American English. Semantic principles are studied, including connotation and denotation, levels of abstraction and language, and context as a determinant of meaning. Usage and structure are taught as they bear on the speaking and writing problems presented by the course. Spelling and vocabulary are stressed.

In the twelfth grade, the study of semantics is continued, as well as usage and structure of English in their relationship to the course. Spelling and vocabulary are taught in context. The history of the English language is surveyed.

REGULAR PROGRAM

The *regular* program may enroll as many as 50 percent of the English students. This group includes those who are not preparing for college or who require only minimal college preparation.

In tenth-grade written work, the initial concentration is on deductively developed descriptive and expository paragraphs, with subjects drawn from both primary experience and literature. Emphasis is on developing competence in the conventions of the language. Précis and paraphrase of library sources are taught. A paper is assigned every 12-class period, and revisions and rewriting are frequent.

The program continues in the eleventh grade with utility writing: business letters, filling in of claims, etc. In addition, assignments include both expository and descriptive themes, with concentration on development of theses with adequate supporting evidence, precise word choice, transition, beginnings, and endings. Here, as in the honors and intensive series, students summarize library sources and work on paraphrase and essay tests. One in-class or out-of-class paper is assigned about every ten class days, for a total of approximately 3,000 words a semester in ten 300- to 400-word papers, including three to five written in class.

Senior composition work continues expository and descriptive themes, with subjects derived from matters of general social concern and from literature. There is concentration on development of an adequate thesis, transition, beginnings, and endings. Précis of library sources, paraphrase, and utility writing (business letters, forms, reports) are continued.

Language studies involve concentration on vocabulary and spelling in the tenth grade. Work is also done on levels of language, as well as on the conventions of usage and structural patterns as related to the writing and speaking demanded by the course.

This work is followed the next year by the adjustment of language level to subject, writer, and audience. Use of concrete terms, as opposed to abstractions, is taught. There is concentration on meaning derived from context. Emphasis on spelling is continued, as is emphasis on the conventions of usage and structural patterns related to the course work.

Twelfth-grade language work in this track includes the study of uses and abuses of connotation in mass media and advertising and use of concrete and specific vocabulary. Conventions of usage are taught, as are structural patterns as related to reading and writing demanded by the course. Spelling also is emphasized.

BASIC PROGRAM

Placement in the *basic* program at the high school (tenth-grade level) is made by the student's counselor. The program is open to all those needing special help in reading and writing.

In written work, the stress is on sentence patterns, with progression to narrative and descriptive paragraphs as students are ready for them. There is concentration on the topic sentence and the gathering of evidence for its development.

This work is continued in the eleventh grade, with emphasis on descriptive and expository paragraphs, including more work on topic sentence and adequate evidence. The students move on to two- or three-paragraph themes as they progress. Utility writing is introduced, including completion of forms, writing of letters ordering merchandise, letters of complaint, completion of accident reports, income tax reports, and the like.

During the final high school year, a course is offered for seniors who have failed one or more semesters of lower-division English and who are recommended for the course by their counselors. Students must maintain satisfactory progress and a high standard of conduct and application to remain in the course.

The writing assignments are devoted primarily to expository and descriptive papers and paragraphs. There is concentration on explaining a process, definition, and advancing a social thesis. Utility writing, such as form filling, business letters, and report making, is included in the course. An in-class or out-of-class paper is assigned every 15 class days.

The language work throughout this sequence is concentrated on elimination of elementary errors of usage. To this is added, during the junior year, practice in listening, such as following directions closely, and in judging television, radio, and movie performances.

It is evident that such a diversified program can go much further toward meeting students' varied needs than can the single course. Once the English teaching staff of a school system has established an appropriate teaching sequence for the junior high and high school grades, it can give some thought to the diversified needs, abilities, and interests of pupils and often develop quite an imaginatively conceived program for bringing out the best in each group of students.

5

Developing a Sequential Program

Leonard Freyman
English and Library Coordinator
Cleveland Heights City School District

RATIONALE FOR THE PROGRAM

Perhaps the most widely criticized aspect of the secondary English program is the teaching of composition, and Cleveland Heights, though more favored than many high schools, had heard many times the same question: "Why can't Johnny write . . . better?" Since the problem of teaching composition is national, many teachers have demanded, "Why not a national attack on this problem? Why not a uniform course of study or composition sequence for the entire nation?"

Harold Martin of the Harvard University Graduate School of Education and the College Entrance Examination Board's Commission on English has answered these queries. At a talk for the Project English Demonstration Center at Euclid Central Junior High School, Dr. Martin emphasized the necessity for each community to tailor its composition sequence to fit its own particular needs. Already committed to the development of a sequential composition program, Cleveland Heights teachers received new impetus from Dr. Martin's talk to take a critical look at the Cleveland Heights school population and to build a course in terms of particular local student needs.

Cleveland Heights High School patrons are from an upper-middle class suburban population. Approximately 85 percent of Heights High graduates matriculate at college, and 50 percent of these students take the College Boards. For a number of years local norms for all standardized tests have been compared with national norms, and the slightly higher scores recorded in Cleveland Heights reinforce Dr. Martin's plea for a local curriculum geared to the local situation.

DETERMINING A SEQUENCE

The problem of organizing a sequential composition program has only recently received national attention, so Cleveland Heights committees found few "ready-made" sequences. Those available were devoted, for the most part, either to the elementary school or to the secondary school; few groups had worked out a K-12 program.

Consequently, after examining the Nebraska Council of Teachers of English curriculum, Clarence Hach's "Needed—A Sequential Program in Composition," [1] Edwin Sauer's sequence in his *Teaching English in the Secondary School*, and Joseph Mersand's "A Series of Steps Leading Up," [2] the committee determined to establish its own sequence. The problem immediately arose as to whether the sequence should be "logically" or "psychologically" based. As study continued and as the committee met with such consultants as Frances Fletcher of National College of Evanston, William West of the State University of New York, Kenneth Wilson of the University of Connecticut, and Paul Diederich of Educational Testing Service, members inclined more and more toward a psychologically oriented sequence based on current findings from growth and development studies. Since the consultants emphasized the importance of a *logical* sequence, but agreed upon the primary role of *motivation* and *psychology,* the committee determined to use human development studies as the base and to overlay on this base the logical, sequential composition learnings.

ESTABLISHING DEVELOPMENTAL GOALS

The Cleveland Heights committee worked for four weeks examining the typical interests, traits, and needs of 5- to 18-year-

---

[1] *English Journal* 49: 536-47; November 1960.
[2] *NEA Journal* 88: 23-25; December 1960.

old pupils in the light of their implications for the language arts. Because of the importance of motivating pupils, the group, working in teams of three with the consultants, concentrated on developing both realistic, achievable developmental goals for each grade level and on designing motivational keys or stimuli to suggest to teachers creative ways of achieving the goals. The goals ranged from one of the kindergarten's, "To release free and genuine self-expression," to one of the twelfth grade's, "To build understanding and appreciation of language through writing general semantics reports distinguishing words and things."

Because of the emphasis on human development, on developmental goals, and on motivation, the committee determined that the format of the finished sequence should reveal these primary aspects. The printed sequential program lists, for each grade level, developmental goals for students of the appropriate age, stimuli (motivational keys), and activities.

CONSTRUCTING ASSIGNMENTS

With the K-12 developmental goals clearly established, the teams began by constructing the specific springboards or stimuli (motivational keys) for writing activities and then developed these activities. For the specific writing assignments, the teams consulted books on teaching composition, published sequences, and literature allocated to each grade level, but they depended primarily upon their own ideas, experience, and ingenuity.

USING LITERATURE AS A SPRINGBOARD

Although the committee recognized the desirability of having students, by writing, re-examine their own experiences, they felt that literature-based composition, particularly at the secondary level, should comprise a large part of the writing assignments. When possible, the committee designed experiences correlating literature and personal experience and uniting them as a foundation for composition. The opportunities for using literature as a springboard for composition are unlimited, and thus composition assignments were based on literature ranging from *Wind in the Willows* in the elementary school to *Hamlet* in the senior high. Brief excerpts from the format for grades 4, 6, and 8 follow.

Sequential Composition Program, K-6
Grade 4

GOAL	STIMULUS	ACTIVITY
To write a friendly letter	Date Greeting Message Closing Name	Learn and practice using the five elements of a friendly letter
To rephrase ideas found in reference books	Use material from social studies, science, *Britannica Junior*, *The World Book* Stress on accurate information, organization, encouragement of manipulation of sentence	Make independent selection of useful, important words and copy for use in a report Reduce a paragraph to a single sentence Summarize one to three pages in a short paragraph
To write a paragraph with a topic sentence	Personal experience Opinion Feeling	Begin with experiences common to all, such as— My birthday party was a big success. Our (family, school) trip to _____ was really an adventure. I felt proud when _____.
	Summary of textbook material for reporting	Five new words in my vocabulary are _____.
	Autobiographical experience	We are a family of (no. in family).
To write main idea of a chapter in a book, one to three sentences	Independent reading Material from social studies, science	Emphasize facts or opinions of author Use this skill in essay-type answers to questions
To write a topic outline using phrases for headings		Outlines based on social science

Grade 6

GOAL	STIMULUS	ACTIVITY
To make a bibliography	Report on recreational reading — *English Is Our Language*	Compile lists of favorite books

GOAL	STIMULUS	ACTIVITY
	Organization or re-organization of room library	Select a theme, such as horses or heroes, and make bibliographies
		List six to eight books by author, title, place of publication, publisher, and date
		Share lists with class
		Prepare a list of books not now in school library that students wish to see purchased
To take notes from reading, listening, observing	Class or school newspaper	Interview a student, friend, or teacher, listing— Who was interviewed Date Questions and answers
	Interview of a story character	Imagine an interview with a character in a story or an imaginary character, such as— Pecos Bill Paul Revere Paul Bunyan A mermaid
	Subject matter film Television at home or school	Report on film or filmstrip, listing— Name or subject of film Main ideas
	Newspaper Magazine Story Poem	Listen to material read by teacher and take notes
	Field trip Science experience	Take notes from science experience or field trip, listing— Subject or reason for trip Date and place Main ideas or learnings
To make a three-step outline using notes	Oral report from topic outline	Use Roman numerals for topics

GOAL	STIMULUS	ACTIVITY
taken from observing, reading, listening		Capital letters for subtopics Arabic numerals for additional details

Sequential Composition Program, 7-12

Grade 8

GOAL	STIMULUS	ACTIVITY
To write a descriptive paragraph	Discussing not only the hastily spoken words of Philip Nolan, who stormed and said, "Damn the United States! I wish I may never hear of the United States again!" but angry words others may have uttered. (What lies behind any angry word, an angrier word, and finally the extreme explosion of anger that ends a friendship? Are people really uncontrolled? Are they pushed by anger into making extreme statements they don't really mean?) See Sandburg's poem "Primer Lesson."	Write in chronological order an incident you remember in which you spoke words in haste or in anger that you were not able to take back.
To study sentence variety through use of compound and complex sentences To reinforce giving reasons or opinions	Reviewing the actions of some of the children in relation to their parents. Centering a discussion around discipline in the home. Asking questions such as the following: How were you brought up? How should boys and girls be punished? Rewarded?	Think about yourself in relation to your friends. Are you satisfied with the relationship? Dissatisfied? Write a composition analyzing these relationships.

GOAL	STIMULUS	ACTIVITY
To reinforce the importance of specificity. To reinforce the importance of order in writing	Learning how Braille was invented; the assembly line was originated; printing was invented.	Choose as a topic something you have done and can do a good job of explaining to someone else.
To analyze statements and quotations for interpretation in oral and written compositions	Sample quotations, such as— "We should pray not for lighter burdens but for stronger backs." — Theodore Roosevelt "Cutting remarks usually are made by people who aren't sharp." — Country Parson "The man who lets himself be bored is even more contemptible than the bore." —Samuel Butler	Analyze and discuss your selected quotation, supporting your thinking by example and exposition.
	Sample statements, such as— "Rhetoric may be defined as discovering the possible means of persuasion in reference to any subject whatever." —Aristotle. "To influence his audience, the speaker needs knowledge of the world."—Cicero "There are some things which depend not on the teacher but on the learner." — Quintilian	Explain your selected statement as clearly and concretely as possible.
To study the classical rhetorical principles of invention (content), disposition (organization), exposition (style), memory	Terms used in classical rhetoric to be defined. Examples: *invention, disposition,* and *exposition*	Define your selected term from the standpoint of classical rhetoric.

GOAL	STIMULUS	ACTIVITY
(remembering, not memorizing), and pronunciation (delivery) in oral and written composition		
To study the classical rhetorical principles of invention (content), disposition (organization)	Classical rhetorical terms to be explained Examples: *memoria, pronunciation*	Explain your selected classical rhetorical term in the light of the modern speech course.

DISTINGUISHING CREATIVE AND EXPOSITORY WRITING

Although college-bound students today need increased work in exposition, the committee felt that creative writing should be encouraged and rewarded, particularly in the primary and elementary grades. Actually, the committee recommends that all writing be "creative," since every sentence "brings into being something that did not before exist." With the attitude toward writing that this label promotes, teachers will regard each child's sincere paper as a creative product worthy of respect.

The committee distinguished, however, between "discursive" writing—that which aims primarily at communicating information—and "nondiscursive" writing—that which aims at communicating personal attitude and emotion. The former can be taught and judged, since it makes use of culturally evolved forms and rhetorical patterns and must convey information effectively, interestingly, and pleasingly. The latter, since it is unique, subjective, and often very personal, is not only difficult to teach but almost impossible to judge.

The sequential composition program provides for both discursive and nondiscursive writing, but suggests that the latter be encouraged and appreciated rather than graded.

FORESEEING THE FUTURE OF THE SEQUENTIAL PROGRAM

Like the textbook which faces revision almost before release, this sequential program is already being re-examined. Currently the staff is working on a thematic program for the senior high

English courses. When this experimental thematic program is introduced, it will probably necessitate the revision and updating of the sequential program. Consequently, the program must be considered tentative, ever ready for revision. Like science, the program contains a built-in commitment to correction; and, like society, it requires constant re-evaluating and updating to meet the needs of a dynamic civilization and an always emerging culture.

6

Literature and Writing

Helen F. Olson
Director, English Language Arts
Seattle Public Schools

During the past year, the first of the participation of Seattle Public Schools in the NEA Composition Project funded by the Dean Langmuir Foundation, emphasis has been placed upon relating ideas found in reading literature to written composition. The idea that reading strengthens speech and writing and that oral and written discussion gives added purpose and meaning to reading is not new to Seattle; it is the central theme of the basic course of study, *Guideposts to the English Language Arts, Kindergarten Through Grade Twelve,* and specific applications are made at each grade level.

The theme readers afforded through the NEA Project have freed teachers from much paper correcting and thus allowed additional time for planning and increased teaching in depth. Another asset has been opportunity for conferences of the participating teachers, of the teachers and theme readers, of individual teachers and theme readers, and of the individual student with his theme reader and teacher. The essential relationship of discriminating reading, thoughtful discussion, and sensitive written composition has emerged as the key emphasis of this year's work.

Perhaps the relationship between reading and writing can best be made clear through a brief description of each of the series of observation lessons presented by eight of the participating teachers, in an effort to share their thinking and experience with others in the Project, with other staff members, and with visitors from other school systems.

Since Seattle is interested in how the work of one grade level prepares for and supports that of the next, teachers of grades 6 through 12 are included; thus our demonstrations have illustrated the teaching of writing at seven different grade levels, elementary through senior high school. Each demonstration has shown one step—or a part of one step—in the basic five-step composition process used in all Seattle classrooms, at all grade levels. This basic process, subject to infinite variations in content and approach, includes all aspects of English language arts and requires on the average about two weeks. The five steps are (a) reading, thinking, and discussing; (b) planning the writing; (c) writing the first draft; (d) proofreading, sharing, revising, rewriting, and evaluating; (e) direct teaching of certain basic skills. Each of the eight observation lessons is preceded and followed by a discussion among the visitors and the demonstrating teacher and theme reader.

Last spring the first two observation lessons were presented by sixth-grade teachers, one in each of the two participating elementary schools. One teacher illustrated Step V of the basic composition process. The pupils had concluded the first four steps, and their papers had been written, shared, proofread, revised, rewritten, and filed in individual folders. This lesson was devoted to teaching a specific skill with which, as the compositions revealed, the pupils needed help. The skill being studied by the class was use of colorful adjectives in descriptions of impressions received through the five senses.

The second grade 6 observation lesson showed the pupils in Step IV. They had written their papers and, this day, were sharing them and discussing them in terms of the criteria they had set for their writing. Recognizing the short attention span of normal sixth graders, the teacher engaged the students in a number of activities, all related to revision of their papers. They used the chalkboard for improving awkward sentences, examined keys to logical development of a topic, shared some of their papers by reading them aloud and by listening to passages read by the teacher, and then discussed ways to improve their descriptive writings.

In the junior high school, the visitors observed three lessons, one in grade 7. Here the teacher, starting with "The Image," by Sylvia Townsend Warner, led the students in an animated discussion of imagery, particularly as related to superstition. From this discussion, the class moved toward notetaking of ideas for their own papers. Next came the development of criteria for their writings, including the use of simile, effective opening, one-idea development, and vivid vocabulary.

The grade 8 lesson was part of a unit on American humorists. The class had been studying surprise endings, exaggeration, understatement, and irony contained in humorous narratives and poems. This day, the class listened to a recording of James Thurber's "The Night the Bed Fell." The story line was discussed briefly. Then the discussion shifted to such subjects as Mr. Thurber's inspiration for his characters and interesting people in everyday life. Preparation for the composition centered on selecting a dominant impression of a personality. The class discussed physical characteristics which can be used in observing people and then compiled a check list to use in taking notes of their own observations.

The grade 9 demonstration lesson concerned Step IV: sharing and revising the students' first drafts. The overhead projector was used to display papers and assist pupils in proofreading. The criteria previously agreed upon were reviewed. Then students were arranged in small groups to help in proofreading and revising one another's papers. During this time, the theme reader and teacher moved freely about the room giving suggestions and answering questions. Previously, through correction of pupils' papers and some conferences with individual pupils, the theme reader had become acquainted with the class. Several papers selected by the various groups were read aloud by the writers and discussed by the class. The sensitive, imaginative descriptions and the maturity of discussion in a heterogeneous grade 9 class gave evidence of the close reading and study of word pictures, of vivid phrasing, and of figurative language upon which the writing lesson had been built.

The grade 10 observation lesson, which was in a class of only average ability, showed Step I of the composition process. The literary work being taught was Robert Frost's "The Death of the Hired Man," and the theme of the discussion was "acceptance and nonacceptance." During the discussion, several previously read works were introduced, among them *Silas Marner* and *The Pearl*. Incidents of acceptance and lack of acceptance were cited by the students. Noteworthy were the teacher's respect for sincere student efforts and the quiet, almost leisurely, approach used to foster thinking. Noteworthy, also, was the fact that the tempo accelerated, rather than diminished, toward the end of the hour. Gradually the class moved toward the assignment to write a composition on the theme—"Am I My Brother's Keeper?" Students were asked to discuss the values and dangers in being one's brother's keeper and to draw upon both reading and personal experience but *not* to use illustrations discussed in class.

The grade 11 observation lesson concerned a class in creative writing, one of the English electives. Students had been reading and discussing short stories and had been considering both the ideas or themes of short stories and the writer's craft in developing his idea. The story read in preparation for this day's discussion was "The Apprentice," by Dorothy Canfield. The discussion considered the various problems involved in creating a story of character: observation, imaginative thinking, vocabulary, plot, setting. Using this story, as well as other stories they had read, as a springboard, the students discussed such matters as (a) what the first paragraph of a story usually does, (b) words used to carry the idea, (c) the power of discriminating repetition, (d) the human relationship established in "The Apprentice," and (e) the relation of the title to a story. In brief, the students were taught principles which could be applied to the writing of their own stories.

During the last observation visitors viewed an unusually able senior class. Students had read, in the days preceding the observation lesson, Sophocles' *Oedipus Rex*, Shakespeare's *Hamlet*, and Miller's *Death of a Salesman*. The discussion centered on the theme: "Is Willy Loman a tragic character?" The writing to follow would deal with some aspect of the question, "What is tragedy?" and each student would develop his theme through consideration of his previous reading, particularly the *Death of a Salesman*.

Perhaps the relationship between written composition and literature can be better understood through examination of two typical lesson plans that were used by the observation-lesson teachers this spring, one at the beginning of the series of demonstrations and one at the end.

GRADE 6:
DEVELOPING THE COMPOSITION PROCESS

The purpose of the observation lesson is to share our experiences during the first semester of our participation in Project Composition. The students are shown one stage of the five-step, basic composition process used in Seattle. The entire composition process usually requires about two weeks and involves learning experiences in all aspects of the English language arts. Following are the steps leading to the present lesson—on understanding our concept of teaching and learning written composition—and those to follow it.

Preceding Lessons

Step I   *Reading and Thinking*

Two and one-half weeks before this lesson, the class was introduced to *Aesop's Fables* through the teacher's reading of several fables. A brief history of fables was discussed prior to the reading. The characteristics of fables, such as the relationship between animals and human beings, the moral concept, the length, and the effective use of direct quotations, were discussed.

Step II   *Planning the Writing*

Characteristics of fables were reviewed, especially the use of colorful verbs. Punctuation in direct quotations was reviewed, and proper page form was stressed. A number of morals from *Aesop's Fables* were placed on the board. Each student chose one about which to write.

Step III   *Writing the First Drafts*

From the beginning of the year, pupils constructed a topic-sentence outline prior to writing the first draft of a paper. For the current fable writing no such requirement was made; therefore, the teacher was able to observe the pupils' organization habits when pupils were acting independently. All went directly into the writing of the first draft.

Step IV   *Evaluating, Revising, Rewriting*

Several pupils read their fables to the class. After each was read, the boys and girls told what they liked about it and also where they felt improvement could be made. Next, they made corrections on their own papers through the use of a directed, step-by-step look at the proofreading chart. The designated proofreading symbols were placed where needed. The final draft was written from the corrected first draft and turned in to the theme reader. She had an opportunity to talk individually with seven students during

the course of this one writing process. More conferences were planned for a later date.

Demonstration Lesson

Step V   *Direct Teaching of Language Skills*

The final step of the composition process is to teach
thoroughly some of the appropriate language skills.
The skills are chosen from those with which the
pupils have difficulty in their written compositions
and from the grade 6 section of *Guideposts to the
English Language Arts.*

This lesson emphasizes the use of colorful adjectives.
The children are shown the importance of adjectives
in effective writing. A short story is then read to the
class, and the pupils identify adjectives.

Colorful adjectives are discussed in relation to the
five senses. Pupils use their own words in describing
nouns written on the blackboard and then write
sentences utilizing colorful language. Several pupils
are asked to read their sentences, leaving out the
noun being discussed. The remainder of the class
attempts to guess what is being described.

Succeeding Lessons

Follow-Up

After some time has been devoted to teaching and
testing certain specific language skills, these skills
will be added to the accumulating list of language
skills to be maintained in future writings. Then the
written compositions will be filed in individual pupil
folders and the class will begin another basic, five-
step composition process.

GRADE 12: LEARNING TO WRITE THROUGH THE COMPOSITION PROCESS

This series of lessons is part of a unit on drama, the unit
title for Advanced Literature being "The Art of Tragedy."
Materials include drama from the early Greeks, from Shakespeare, and from contemporary American playwrights. In addition, prose selections relating to the nature and theory of tragedy
will be studied. Each entire composition process, including some
reading and discussion, requires about two weeks.

Preceding Lessons

Step I   *Reading and Thinking Together*

Reading and discussion of Sophocles' *Oedipus Rex*
Reading and discussion of William Shakespeare's
Hamlet

Reading and discussion of Arthur Miller's *Death of a Salesman*

Demonstration Lesson

Step II   *Discussing and Planning the Writing*

In this lesson we begin a discussion of *Death of a Salesman,* which we have read and have seen performed by the Seattle Repertory Theatre. During the next few lessons, we will explore some of the play's ideas, note the means by which these ideas are conveyed, and consider their theatrical and social significance.

To understand something of the unique effect of tragedy upon us, we will compare the means and ends of this play with those of plays we have previously studied (*Oedipus Rex, Oedipus at Colonus, Antigone, Hamlet*). As a frame of reference, we will refer to Aristotle's *Poetics*, accepting or modifying his views through close critical examination.

Through this discussion we are seeking neither unanimity nor absolute certainty. Rather, we are attempting to discover and articulate some tentative, flexible sense of form and order in this play as an artistic entity and in its ideas as relevant philosophy. If we bring any bias to our discussion it is that this is a moving, important work of art and what it is and says is worth our serious consideration.

Following our discussion we will write an essay, the subject of which will be determined by what remains to be said and by what will best stimulate individual thought.

Succeeding Lessons

Step III   *Writing the First Draft*

Reviewing the criteria accumulated during the semester for evaluating written work.

Writing the essay.

Proofreading compositions and revising and rewriting them in terms of the criteria agreed upon.

Submitting the compositions to the theme reader for correction.

Step IV   *Evaluating the Writing; Then Filing Compositions in Individual Student Folders*

Returning to the students the compositions corrected by the theme reader and discussing the strengths and weaknesses called to the attention of the students by the theme reader.

Sharing the papers and discussing them, gaining points of evaluation and suggestions for improvement from one another; for instance, commenting on effective sentences and aptly used verbals.

Having some especially effective papers read aloud.

Assigning the final revision and rewriting of the papers as homework.

Filing the corrected and now graded papers in the individual student folders.

Step V   *Teaching the Language Skills*

Writing samples of poorly worded sentences on the board and encouraging suggestions from students as to how to improve them.

Teaching, reteaching, and testing other points of grammar, punctuation, usage, and spelling which caused errors in the compositions; teaching to the entire group those skills which seem most to be needed by the majority of the class.

Checking the list of language skills allocated for grade 12 in *Guideposts to the English Language Arts* to make certain that all in the list have been thoroughly taught by the end of the year.

Evidence of the achievements of students six years from now will be available, for the Seattle English Language Arts Department intends to keep the participating students, who number about 2,200 this year, together through high school and to observe their progress in college or on the job after high school.

7

Using
the New
Linguistics

Elwood Prestwood
Assistant Superintendent
Lower Merion School District

Still one of the basic issues in the teaching of English is the question of how writing should be taught. Few teachers admit to being satisfied with the present quality of student writing; consequently, many are seeking effective ways of attacking the problem. To date, there is little agreement as to the best way of improving student writing.

The Lower Merion teachers participating in the NEA Engglish Composition Project are among those who are much concerned about the problem of improving the quality of student writing. Like many others, they have turned toward the "new" linguistics as a means of attacking the difficulties they sense. Aware of the divergent views among the linguists, conscious of Gleason's statement that "one of the peculiar blind spots of linguists is [their] failure to give much attention to written language," [1] and acquainted with Laird's caution regarding the need to be an expert to deal with the complications of the study

---

[1] Gleason, H. A., Jr. "What Is English?" *Linguistics, Composing, and Verbal Learning.* p. 9.

of the structure of the English language,[2] the Lower Merion teachers dared to explore linguistics to find at least a partial answer to their problems. They accepted Francis' statement that "linguistics is a science . . . while composition is either a skill or an art, or both." [3] They wondered, however, whether the science of linguistics can serve to improve the quality of student writing just as science is useful in increasing production and quality control in the workaday world of industry. Consequently, they used *Structural Grammar in the Classroom* by Verna L. Newsome (published by Wisconsin Council of Teachers of English, 3700 North 75th Street, Milwaukee 16, Wisconsin) as a basis for their explorations of the usefulness of linguistics. The discussion that follows is not a brief for or against the new linguistics.

Despite the belief voiced by Roberts that linguistic science has no cure for the problems of the composition class,[4] the Lower Merion teachers did learn that structural grammar can make several contributions to the improvement of student writing. They also learned that the degree of effectiveness of the contributions depends upon the skill of the individual teacher.

An essential principle of linguistics is that the study of language "begins with the features of form and structure, then proceeds to the use or function of these features, and only then goes on to the consideration of the meaning." [5] Linguistics emphasizes that the English language secures its structure from the spoken language. Consequently, one of the first contributions that the Lower Merion teachers recognized linguistics could make to the writing program was directly related to the use of oral language—having students realize that in speaking they employ sentence patterns useful in their writing. Using an inductive approach, a teacher can soon fill a chalkboard with examples that his pupils can give from their own speech. Through observation and the help of the instructor, the students can recognize that there are many differences in the structure of the sentences that they use in everyday conversations. The

[2] Laird, Charlton. "Structural Linguistics: Notes for a Devil's Advocate." *College English* 24: 93; November 1962.

[3] Francis, W. Nelson. "Linguistics and Written Composition." *Language, Linguistics, and School Programs.* p. 95.

[4] Roberts, Paul. "Linguistics and the Teaching of Composition." *English Journal* 52: 333; May 1963.

[5] Allen, Harold B. "Linguistics and Written Composition." *Language, Linguistics, and School Programs.* p. 85.

teacher can deliberately point to the values of using those differences in written composition and can teach his students the different patterns with a view to incorporating them in their writing. From this beginning the students can be led to work out the formulas of the sentence patterns identified by the linguists and subsequently to utilize the patterns in their own compositions. Through this approach the instructor can use the principle of going from what is known to what is unknown, thereby improving the effectiveness of the learning to be achieved.

While using the oral language as a basis for the presentation of sentence patterns, the instructor can stress that in speech students can and do convey meaning through the intonations made by their voice. On paper these intonations are diminished or lost, and sometimes these losses result in ambiguities. Through the employment of sentences illustrating the differences that can occur between spoken and written discourse, students can be helped to see that writing is more constraining than speech, that more care must be taken in writing than in speech to avoid ambiguities, and that sentences at times must be reconstructed to eliminate any chance of misinterpretation resulting from the use of a pattern that may be satisfactory in oral language. Lees illustrates this kind of problem very effectively in considering the innocent-looking sentence "John looked over the new desk." [6]

Student writing can be improved not only by eliminating any ambiguities that may exist but also by improving the effectiveness of sentence structure of expressions that do convey meaning, no matter how poorly they may be written. Some linguists have shown how a linguistic knowledge of the structure of a sentence can help students make marked improvement in their writing. Borgh feels that students who are aware of the sentence patterns identified by the linguists can use that knowledge in eliminating errors which are not very obvious. One of her illustrations shows how the application of Pattern III (Noun—Linking Verb—Noun) to "The reason for this is women competing with men" assisted a pupil in seeing the lack of logic in what he had written.[7] Allen, in an article already referred to, devotes two pages to showing in a point-by-point procedure how linguistic knowledge can aid a student to revise "Later on

[6] Lees, Robert B. "The Promise of Transformational Grammar." *English Journal* 52: 329-30; May 1963.

[7] Borgh, Enola M. *Grammatical Patterns and Composition.* p. 6.

we made a list of all the words which are pronounced the same and are spelled differently each having a different meaning" in such a way that he can develop three meaningful sentences, any one of which would be highly acceptable.[8]

Many teachers spend some time in having students identify parts of speech in sentences. A thorough understanding of the patterns of sentences as analyzed by the linguists helps students immeasurably in this type of exercise by showing how position offers clues. To demonstrate that the place of a word in a sentence can determine the part of speech, some teachers use nonsense words. For example, most students with a knowledge of sentence patterns can readily classify the nonsense words in the following sentence: *Doiles like amet* (possible translation: Dogs like meat). By working with the sentence patterns, students can learn how the parts of speech (noun, pronoun, verb, adjective, adverb) accepted by most linguists function in specific positions in sentences.

The linguistic approach also uses signals other than position in the classification of words, signals which can be utilized without the benefit of the lexical meaning of words. In the nonsense sentence which follows, students have little difficulty in inductively seeing that the group of words conveys a grammatical meaning (not thought): *The mations crickled the lolls*. They can be shown that each of the unfamiliar "words" has at least one way of signaling its part of speech. First of all, position reveals that *mations* and *lolls* are nouns, that *crickled* is a verb as found in Pattern IV (Noun—Transitive Verb—Noun) in Newsome's system of classification. Two other signals—the derivational suffix *-ion* and the plural inflection *-s*—indicate that *mations* is a noun. *Lolls* has the plural inflection of a noun. *Crickled* is signaled as a verb by the *-ed* past tense inflectional ending and by the derivational suffix *-le*. An exercise using nonsense words adds emphasis to the reasons for knowing affixes and inflectional endings. This knowledge can be used by students in improving their writing.

The nonsense sentence uses a fourth signal—the structure word *the*, which always signals a noun. According to the linguist, all words which cannot be classified by the formal signals which identify noun, pronoun, verb, adjective, and adverb are placed in the category of structure words.[9] This designation has helped some students to overcome the difficulties at times encountered

---

[8] Allen, *op. cit.*, p. 89.

[9] Newsome, Verna L. *Structural Grammar in the Classroom*. p. 6.

in understanding the conventional definitions of *preposition* and *conjunction*. For example, if a student understands that a preposition is a structure word that signals that a nominal (noun or pronoun) known as the object follows, he can see that a word like *of* or *with* signals that an object should usually follow and he looks for (if he is analyzing a sentence) or places (if he is writing his own sentence) an object after the signaling word. Some teachers succeed in having students sense rather quickly why the objective case pronoun should be used after *of* or *with*, even when they do not know the traditional definition of the preposition.

Perhaps the most valuable contribution linguistics can make to the improvement of student writing results from the help it can give pupils in developing a mature style. Style, as Newsome points out, depends upon the choice of words and the way they are put together.[10] Structural linguistics is concerned with the way words are put together. In this phase of instruction the Lower Merion teachers begin with the shortest sentences of each pattern as classified by Newsome and help students understand how each can be expanded by using coordination and all kinds of modifiers. Constantly during the instruction the students are reminded about the basic patterns and how the additions relate to the component parts of the patterns. Through the gradual expansion of each pattern in exercises designed to aid students in their understanding of what can be done and through the teacher's having them expand their sentences in their compositions, students learn about style and its relationship to meaning and maturity of thought. Probably this aspect of instruction, if the teacher has the necessary background information, can include use of Chomsky's transformational grammar.[11]

As students learn to expand their sentences, they can be made aware of the many structural choices that are available to express their thoughts. As Fries said in 1940 in *American English Grammar,* what distinguishes the writing of educated people from that of the uneducated is the greater control of syntactic resources of the language the educated person has.[12] According to Allen, students can learn about and use in their writing replacement potentials with great effectiveness if in-

[10] Newsome, Verna L. "Expansions and Transformations To Improve Sentences." *English Journal* 53: 327-28; May 1964.

[11] Chomsky, Noam. *Syntactic Structures.* New York: Gregory Lounz, Books, 1957. 116 pp.

[12] Allen, *op. cit.,* p. 87.

struction "is premised upon sound linguistic information."[13]

Another contribution linguistics can make to student writing grows out of the emphasis it places upon spoken language as it relates to usage. An acceptance of linguistic science findings forces one to recognize that there are different dialects or levels of usage and that each is correct if used under appropriate conditions. A student can be led to see that his written discourse can be inappropriate if he uses a dialect not suited to his purpose, his situation, and his intended audience. The study of language as employed in the United States should help students improve their writing as they prepare for the future they intend to make for themselves. A college-bound student, for example, should recognize what dialect or dialects affect his speech and what aspects of them he may be able to use in writing in college.

Since linguistics compels one to pay close attention to oral language, it can help students realize that the pitch, stress, and juncture indicated by the voice cannot easily be transferred to paper. One means available to them for accomplishing necessary transfers is punctuation. Although grammatical structure plays an important part in the punctuation of prose, particularly of expository writing, students can secure clues for some punctuation through paying attention to intonational patterns that are part of their spoken language.

Although lessening hostility toward writing, and particularly toward the study of grammar, may not be classified as a direct contribution to improving student compositions, the linguistic approach does tend to cause students to react more positively to writing assignments.[14] Several of the Lower Merion teachers found during the past year that even the slow-learning students developed much more interest in writing than similar students had done in the past. Although they have no statistical proof as yet, the instructors believe that these pupils also improved their writing at a faster rate than past experience indicated they would do.

Obviously this chapter is incomplete in its presentation of the contributions linguistics can make to the improvement of student writing. The science of linguistics is constantly expanding our knowledge about the English language. Teachers should be alert to use any help linguistics may provide in meeting the problems inherent in improving the quality of student writing.

---

[13] *Ibid.*

[14] Link, Frances R., and Schuster, Edgar H. "Linguistics in High School." *Educational Leadership* 19: 297; February 1962.

8

I Am a Theme Reader

Joan First
Theme Reader
*Lansing Public Schools**

Who am I? How can I help?

I am a theme reader, a kind of lay assistant to a profes-sional, experienced English teacher. For 10 months I helped to make a stepped-up high school composition program possible. Other theme readers have done the same tasks, rendered the same assistance, with much the same results. Let me tell you my story.

Last school year I read more than 1,500 high school English themes. Total time invested: 150 hours.

Any energetic English teacher might match this record. What makes it distinctive is that I am not—nor have I been—

* Joan First received her B.A. degree from Michigan State University in 1956. She majored in journalism. Mrs. First served as education reporter for the *Saginaw News* in 1957 and was a full-time staff writer for the *Michigan Education Journal* during the years 1959-61. At present, Mrs. First is a part-time editorial consultant for the Michigan Home Economic Cooperative Extension Service, does free-lance writing, and is city govern-ment reporter for the *East Lansing Towne Courier*.

a classroom teacher. I am a trained journalist. My professional education and experience have been keyed to the concise, colorful brand of communication which characterizes the mass media.

As a theme reader employed in the NEA-supported project in Lansing, Michigan, I freed one teacher at Eastern High School from much of his job of theme grading. At the same time I exposed sophomore and senior English students to new criteria for written communication.

Students participating in the NEA-Langmuir Project wrote one theme every week. The resulting stack of nearly 90 papers, added to the regular teacher's full teaching load and the responsibility for supervision of Eastern's student publications, would have created an impossible drain on his "free" time.

What happens when an unfamiliar, and by traditional standards unqualified, adult enters the two-sided student-teacher relationship? Would I be able to communicate to students my own zest for writing—and my respect for conciseness, directness, and honesty of approach? Would my presence in the classroom of a veteran teacher be positive or negative? Would my own professional ego take a beating? These are some of the questions which the NEA Project posed for me. Here are some of the answers.

In a preschool conference the teacher with whom I worked discussed with me the year ahead and laid some ground rules. Initially, his interest in publications and my past experience as an education writer helped establish rapport.

Soon the basic problem of my role as a reader emerged. Sophomore and senior students would devote one class session weekly to theme writing. Writing would be done in the classroom with adult assistance readily available. As often as possible, I would be at Eastern on writing days. This meant I received the week's assignment with the students, making accurate criticism of their papers possible. (If I could not be in the classroom personally, I received the assignment later from the teacher by telephone, and the themes came to my home via a student friend.)

Once the assignment was made, I stationed myself in an adjoining room with the previous week's papers. One at a time students came in, picked up their papers, reviewed comments and penciled in corrections, and discussed the resulting grade. Usually the teacher distributed part of each set of papers. This gave him an opportunity to see a portion of each week's themes and to observe my handling of them.

During theme distribution, I encouraged students to defend themselves if they felt their grade was unfair. Often a student-teacher-reader discussion was held; sometimes review of the situation favored the student's viewpoint.

During the reading, each paper was assigned two grades. The first related directly to content, the student's approach to the subject, quality of communication, and his understanding of the assignment. The second was based upon the mechanics of writing. While discussing papers with students, I emphasized reasons for the first grade. I sought to contribute little as a grammarian.

As my own relationships with students developed, my confidence in arriving at the more subjective grade grew accordingly. In a one-to-one relationship, youngsters were eager to talk about their feelings about writing, their academic and social frustrations, and their parental pressures and—particularly the seniors—about the future. For many of them, writing was a highly personal experience, and their themes yielded a wealth of insight about their abilities and their problems. In two instances, theme subject matter repeatedly seemed to indicate serious adjustment problems. These were passed on at once to the experienced teacher and counselor.

As writing experience accumulated, each set of themes yielded examples of exceptionally fine, expressive handling of the language. I made notes of these as I read the themes and at the beginning of the class hour wrote particularly polished sentences and phrases on the chalkboard. This both provided good examples and gave individual recognition. Surprisingly enough, the real gems often came from youngsters who would not have received favorable attention had the emphasis been on the mechanics of writing.

The more flexible side of my job—the at-home reading hours—fell into a less stable pattern. Two preschool youngsters and a baby, who arrived in early December, complicated the picture considerably. Once the first semester was well underway, my own "free" time vanished. Theme reading went on several evenings a week from the time the last child fell asleep until *I* fell asleep. During peak periods the very early morning hours became a time resource. One batch of 90 papers was read in the comparatively peaceful surroundings of a local maternity ward.

If the burden of reading these papers had fallen upon the classroom teacher, it would have absorbed time he needed for class preparation as well as for the continued learning and recreational activities that permit a teacher to function optimally.

To me, however, the job represented a break from routine rather than an extension of it. At the same time I became aware that I was in my own field at a new, very basic level.

To the teacher considering use of a reader, clearly the freedom from paper work will loom as the greatest benefit. We found there were fringe benefits, too: the theme reader's appearance in the classroom gives prestige to "writing day" for students. It offers a break in routine and an opportunity for some adult conversation and problem sharing for the teacher.

While my initial relationship with the teacher began with emphasis on our similarities of interest, I am sure pupils benefited most from our differences. For example, while the teacher's personal interest in music and photography stimulated the imagination of some pupils, my own fascination with drama and my avid reading habits sparked others. One Lansing reader, once a professional folksinger, shared her enthusiasm in the classroom, and a study of ballad forms resulted.

The year that began in skepticism ended in satisfaction. I offered my time, my interest, and a sense of responsibility to a teacher. He accepted it willingly and with respect for its worth. We feel certain that the students benefited.

In almost any community there are people like me, able and willing to help make the teaching of composition more interesting and effective. When the burden of teaching English becomes too heavy, let us give you a hand. Together, we can do the job.

9

Writing and the Average Student

Elsa R. Graser
Director of the Project
Baltimore Public Schools

In September 1963, when the Baltimore City Public Schools joined the NEA Project in Composition, the Baltimore center's purpose was to help its average boys and girls write better. The average Baltimore student is not "culturally different," "culturally deprived," or even "inner city"; nor is he "college-bound" or "academically talented." He may be inactive mentally but he possesses latent ability that must be aroused. He may achieve at a below-average level because he lacks motivation. He may never be a leader; he can be the solid force supporting some leader's dynamic drive. And many of Baltimore's 180,000 students are like him.

To try to reach this average slow-learning student, the center selected four tenth-grade classes at Patterson High School in industrial East Baltimore and four seventh-grade classes at Lemmel Junior High School, in a north-central residential area. Each of these schools was assigned two teachers and provided with eight nonschool theme readers from the Langmuir grant. The goal for these classes was clear: more fluent, accurate, and responsible writing. Standardized test results, tabulated in the appendix to this chapter, show that these children of parents in unskilled, semiskilled, or skilled occupations are indeed average and are not well equipped to reach this goal. Their first writing revealed the weakness in thought, structure, diction, and mechanics that the test results had predicted.

This year the center has been analyzing the weaknesses and exploring ways to correct them. Students in some of the classes have written as many as 26 paragraphs. To the teachers, the paragraph was of primary importance, because having to say something about a dominant idea might produce better sentences. In each paragraph, theme readers sought something to commend and some concrete improvement to suggest. At first they ignored poor spelling and sentence structure, hoping that students unshowered with red ink might become more confident. But readers, and teachers, too, came to feel that tacit overlooking of errors encouraged students also to overlook them. Now, although the readers do note gross errors, they still comment chiefly on organization and ideas.

Although the students grasped the content of stories and articles suited to their reading levels, they were baffled by trying to combine writing with the discussion of implications, inferences, and motives. Teachers therefore decided to relate writing assignments to the students' experiences rather than to literature. Students worked with directions, still keeping the paragraph the basic unit. When three students, following incomplete and inexact directions, developed three different diagrams, the group learned that irresponsible writing is inefficient. The classes recorded simple experiments performed before them. They reported staged interruptions in the lesson that demanded quick, accurate observation. They described pens, pencils, their homes and fellow students, and even their teacher. When one class described an old-fashioned carving-knife holder so accurately that the theme reader, who had never seen one, could tell what they were describing, the class knew it had written well.

No opportunity for writing was overlooked. Tenth-grade classes, having visited the Social Security Buildings near Baltimore to learn of vocational opportunities, wrote of the trip. Seventh graders wrote notes to absent teachers and reactions to noisy cafeterias and an epidemic of fighting. They answered essay questions for history and described experiments for science. Toward the end of the year, all classes returned with some success to writing assignments based on their reading, as they described characters from books and collected their book reviews into a pamphlet for the library.

To help these average students learn how to write, the teachers have tried many methods, finding some more successful than others.

The visual approach has been very helpful. Filmstrips helped to make abstractions about sentence fragments concrete; pictures illustrated unity and plan; situation films ending "What should Joe do?" started talk of alternative actions, to be defended in writing. Overhead projectors gave these students what they need: repeated examples of what makes good and bad writing. The projector requires careful use, for illegibility and insufficient screen size may limit projection of some paragraphs. Nevertheless, the projector spotlighted errors, irrelevancies, misplaced ideas, and good writing.

Attempts at group teaching seemed less successful with these boys and girls. Grouping in small units for special work demanded an individual responsibility for working without supervision that these average classes have not yet developed. In one crowded school where each likely and unlikely area has already become a classroom, no space remained for combining classes even when their English periods coincided. When two seventh-grade classes were combined once a week on the auditorium stage, individuals happily dissolved into group anonymity. The "She knows who you are" of a seating chart maintained some involvement; but these students respond best to constant personal stimulation.

Students and teachers both pleaded for more time. Average students write slowly; they revise even more slowly and, for the most part, without interest, because they don't like puzzles. Responses to questionnaires indicate that most of them believe revision helped them but that many also believe that revision should involve correcting only obvious errors. Finding time to check revisions and arrange the conferences which most students found helpful was very difficult; without the readers, it would have been impossible.

Very early in the year, the fact that these boys and girls, white and Negro, use language far from standard became clear. To them, the final -s on nouns and verbs has never become an informational sign; even when the subject is not masked by a prepositional phrase but immediately precedes the verb, they write "The reader come every week." They use heterodox past and past participle forms (one boy wanted to be told "how good I done") ; many of them regularly omit a final -*ed* in both speaking and writing, not only in an understandable assimilation like "he use to" but even when no infinitive follows. Use of variants or complete omission of the *to be* forms recurs in speaking and writing, especially among the Negro boys and girls.

Conscious of such weaknesses and of the students' lack of fluency, the program's teacher-in-charge met the four seventh-grade classes once a week, combining two classes, to work with material from Roberts and Newsome. Although one class in particular found the sessions neither interesting nor valuable, most students liked the nonsense sentences, accepted words as symbols of meaning, and enjoyed making their own code. Those to whom *Jabberwocky* was new, as it was to most, agreed that it could be English but that *Gaudeamus Igitur* could not. They came to play with sentences more freely, and one boy with real flair triumphantly illustrated a Form Class 4 word with "The girl walked slew-footed."

In two areas especially, these sessions showed how their slow mental perception makes it difficult for these boys and girls to write. "Mail slips out" was not ambiguous to them: the first meaning they saw was the only meaning. Similarly, the first version of a sentence remained the only possible version. Their difficulty in recognizing sentence patterns in expanded forms illustrated how seldom they grasp the elements common in apparently discrete groups.

Observing their language habits showed how close is the tie between their speaking and their writing. They write sounds, not words. What they write is what they hear, but what they hear is often neither standard nor clearly perceived. They hear, say, and write "Yesterday I try on a dress." The boy who used "another words" as a transition was reproducing familiar sounds that he had never linked to meaningful words; he takes things "for granite." These students also have difficulty in writing because they enunciate and project their words poorly. Perhaps making someone hear clearly one's individual words is irrelevant when ideas are not discussed because only action is important; but when someone has never heard a sound clearly, he cannot reproduce it. Furthermore, these students do not link letters to sound: they read *wasp* as *waps*, a familiar pronunciation, and *cannibal* as *cannonball*.

For them, bad thinking, bad speaking, and bad reading make bad writing. This year's observation hints that better writing may make better reading. Alert seventh-grade counselors commented that scores in tests of reading ability given in the second semester showed a greater gain among the writing group than in other seventh-grade classes. For the writing classes, the median gain over the sixth-grade level was 0.83 month; for eight other classes, it was 0.66; for all twelve classes, it was 0.74. A test of the difference between the writing and the other groups suggests, however, that the difference is not statistically significant. Nevertheless, the time given to composition in these four classes limited their amount of reading instruction. If they could gain in reading ability even as much as the other groups, one might guess that organizing ideas for writing reinforces recognition of organization in reading. Further study of the data, especially of the relation of IQ to reading gain, may uncover differences that will be significant.

One interesting observation made during the year concerned the way the classes reacted to their readers. They liked having a reader; three out of four indicated that they would prefer the teacher-reader combination to the teacher alone. They enjoyed the reader's attention in conferences, they waited for her comments on their papers, and they were pleased that somebody was reading what they had written. Whenever readers rated papers, the students accepted the rating as valid, and they knew when their papers were better.

These 250 boys and girls believe they are improving. They have told their counselor, "I think it helps me. Now I know what to look for when I read a paragraph and what to put in it when I write one." Like the students, teachers and readers see progress. Slow but perceptible, it comes from instruction that moves from unity through fullness of idea toward exactness of expression. It comes from practice, which makes writing less physically burdensome, finding something to say less difficult, and organizing material more habitual. It comes from attention, which increases self-esteem and self-respect. Many of these boys and girls are enjoying success for perhaps the first time.

This first year's work has improved but certainly not perfected these average students' writing. It has also indicated the next step. In 1964-65, in six schools throughout Baltimore, 24 "average" eighth- and eleventh-grade classes (these groups are likely to remain intact for observation the following year) will be studied. Both eighth- and eleventh-grade experimental groups will move through the same sequence of composition principles, working for organization and content. The program will attempt to isolate and measure whatever improvements in writing these boys and girls show from having a reader, or from writing every week or every other week, or from approaching writing by way of speaking.

Some 1,100 average Baltimore students will be working hard, and they and their teachers ought to learn a great deal about improving writing ability for average students.

STEP TEST RESULTS— SEPTEMBER 1963 AND JUNE 1964

SEVENTH-GRADE EXPERIMENTAL GROUP

Table I:

Class Median Scores for Students Tested Twice

Class	Number	Fall '63 (Form 3A)	Spring '64 (Form 3B)
7-5	31	255	260
7-121	28	250	262-4
7-132	37	253	264
7-212	25	261	272

Table II:

Group Scores for 121 Students Tested Twice

Scores and Norms	Fall '63	Spring '64
Median Score	255	266
Norms: Publisher's Individual Scores*		
Median Score	260	266
Percentile Band for Experimental Group Median Score	28-49	37-64
Mean Score	256.05	264.21
Norms: Publisher's School Mean*		
Average School Mean	259	266
Frequency Percentile of Experimental Group Mean Score	19	31

* Fall '63 scores are compared to publisher's norms for seventh-grade fall testing; spring '64 scores are compared to publisher's norms for eighth-grade fall testing.

TENTH-GRADE EXPERIMENTAL GROUP

Table I:

Class Median Scores for Students Tested Twice

Class	Number	Fall '63 (Form 2A)	Spring '64 (Form 2B)
10-5	24	266	280
10-6	25	275	283
10-7	29	271	277
10-8	25	268	284

Table II:

Group Scores for 103 Students Tested Twice

Scores and Norms	Fall '63	Spring '64
Median Score	271	281
Norms: Publisher's Individual Score*		
Median Score	277	283
Percentile Band for Experimental Group Median Score	25-52	29-58
Mean Score	271.10	279.53
Norms: Publisher's School Mean*		
Average School Mean	277	281
Frequency Percentile of Experimental Group Mean Score	5	20 (score: 279)
		25 (score: 280)

* Fall '63 scores are compared to publisher's norms for tenth-grade fall testing; spring '64 scores are compared to publisher's norms for eleventh-grade fall testing.

TENTH- AND SEVENTH-GRADE EXPERIMENTAL GROUP

Table I:

Gains or Losses on Spring 1964 Test Scores

Class	Number	% Gaining	Average Gain (Points)	% Losing	Average Loss (Points)	% Static
10-5	24	70.83	14.47	20.41	8.2	8.33
10-6	25	84	11.95	8	2	8
10-7	29	65.51	11.84	31.03	7.44	3.44
10-8	25	88	12.95	12	10	
7-5	31	70.96	9.23	25.48	7.87	3.22
7-121	28	78.57	13.36	21.42	8.33	
7-132	37	81.08	13.70	18.91	5.57	
7-212	25	72	15.61	24	7.33	4

SIGNIFICANCE OF DATA SECURED FROM STEP TEST SCORES

Although the tabulation of gains and losses shows clearly that not all students recorded gains in the spring testing, apparently the brighter the class the greater is the percentage of the students recording gains. Of the tenth-grade groups, 10-6 and 10-8 had a higher IQ median than the other two groups in the fall tabulation. The 7-212 class, higher in median IQ in the fall tabulation, lost its brighter students in a regrouping of pupils at the beginning of the second semester and is now more like the three other seventh-grade classes, whose pattern of gains or losses it follows.

Comparison of the scores shows, however, a general improvement, and both tenth- and seventh-grade groups much more nearly approximated the publisher's norms in the spring testing. Particularly noticeable is the tenth-grade mean score movement from the fifth frequency percentile to the twentieth frequency percentile.

Through the kindness of Dean Forbes, specialist in the Educational Testing Services of the Baltimore City Public Schools, the following items were computed for the STEP Test scores for September 1963 and June 1964: the means, the mean gains, the standard deviation, the standard error, the standard error of the difference between the fall and spring scores, and the correlation between the fall and spring scores for both the seventh- and the tenth-grade groups. When the differences in scores were tested with the Critical Ratio, at both grades the differences were found to be highly significant. Because the Critical Ratio equalled 5.499 and 8.051, respectively, the level of probability for these gains is better than 0.01.

The publishers of the STEP writing tests say that they "seek to measure comprehensively the full range of skills involved in the process of good writing." Moreover, they suggest using "one form of STEP Writing at the beginning of the year to assess students' writing abilities and the equivalent form as an end-of-year test to evaluate outcomes." If these claims for the test scores are accepted as indications of writing ability, the work accomplished in both the tenth- and seventh-grade groups shows statistically significant improvement in writing ability.

10

A Summer Program

Stressing Logic and Rhetoric

Elsa R. Graser
Director of the Project
Baltimore Public Schools

Jerome Bruner, in *The Process of Education,* calls the basic ideas in all disciplines simple—as simple as they are powerful—and says that to be in command of these requires a continuous deepening of understanding that comes from learning to use them in progressively more complex forms. A Project English demonstration at the Office of Education early in 1964 emphasized three such basic concepts in composition: isolating the message, giving form to it, and transmitting it. The Baltimore center of the NEA Project Composition is trying to help the average student grasp these concepts. The student who grasps the relation between these principles is beginning to compose, and the earlier he begins, the sooner he will use the more complex forms.

The lessons described here were planned for one-hour demonstration sessions during the Baltimore center's three-week institute of composition in July 1964. Studying the lessons were 45 Baltimore City girls and boys who were to enter the seventh grade in September and who had been selected by their elementary school principals as "average"—not above grade level in reading and in the 90-105 IQ band. It was hoped that through these lessons entering seventh graders might begin to grasp and use the three fundamental concepts.

To isolate the message, the class had to recognize a single purpose, form generalizations that expressed the relation between separate thoughts, and distinguish generalizations from supporting specific details. To form the message, the students had to seek material in their own observations and in reports of other people's observations and to select an effective method for showing the relation of the specifics to the generalization and for fastening them into a cohesive whole. To transmit the message, they had to see their reader clearly, approach him consistently, and affect him deliberately. The following series of lessons was planned to help these seventh graders develop composition skill through seeing inductively or perhaps even intuitively what happens in communication when logic frames the message and rhetoric transmits it. They saw and then they wrote.

LESSON I[1]

Objective: Developing the concept that all writing has a purpose—to focus on a single idea

Show the purpose in different kinds of communication

VISUAL COMMUNICATION

The teacher drew a caricature of herself, exaggerating the obvious features for easy recognition. The class understood the economy of line and related it to the purpose of the caricature.

Cartoons from *Punch* and *The New Yorker* were shown. After the class saw the point of each cartoon, they discussed what each line contributed to making that point.

VISUAL COMMUNICATION WITH WORDS ADDED

Effective advertisements with pictures and some text were shown. The class identified the purpose and related the details of picture and text to the purpose.

VERBAL COMMUNICATION

After the teacher retold the fable of Proserpina, the class decided why the myth had been made and related each detail of the story to that purpose.

The class agreed that all these kinds of communication have a single purpose to which every detail contributes.

---

[1] The lessons which follow are only illustrative. Additional lessons in this program may be obtained from Elsa R. Graser, Baltimore Public Schools, Administration Building Annex, 2521 North Charles Street, Baltimore, Maryland 21218.

Picture advertisements from which all text had been removed were shown. The students determined a purpose for the pictures and wrote a caption or some brief text to emphasize that purpose. They compared their text to the originals and determined which better suited the purpose of the advertisement.

LESSON II

Objective: Further developing the concept of singleness of purpose

Show that the total is more than the parts

A *New Yorker* cover was used to show that the class could discover its date. It showed trees with autumn-colored foliage, two children at the bottom of a winding road, and a tiny orange school bus at the top. When it was shown first with the bus concealed, the students recognized the season from the color of the leaves but couldn't tell what the children were doing. When the bus was uncovered, they spotted the color of a school bus, saw that the children were waiting to be picked up, and correctly dated the cover in September.

A girl was asked how she could tell how many new clothes she might buy. The class decided that the total of her resources—piggy bank, birthday money, allowance—would be more important than any single amount available.

The class discussed what would happen if a group wanted to buy a basketball. It decided that the total of all the boys' contributions would be the important factor.

The class was asked whether it would rather see an All-Star baseball game or an Oriole-Yankee game. It decided that individual brilliance is less interesting than the sureness of a well-unified team.

The class located *E Pluribus Unum* on coins and discussed its meaning, significance as a national motto, and relevance to the idea being illustrated: the total is more than its parts.

Show that the total—the common element—varies with the parts

A single picture was shown on a flannel board. Then others were added, one at a time. As each additional picture was included, the class was asked, "What do they all add up to now?" Three series were shown:

> Poppies, mixed flowers, goldenrod, and ears of corn
> Watermelon cubes, mixed fruit, strawberry tart, ice cream
> Cake, pie, ice cream and cake, ham, breakfast cereal

A single boy was asked to stand. The question, "What do they all add up to now?" was asked after additional individuals were included in the group: first a second boy, then a girl, a teacher, a principal, a parent, a policeman.

Show that the total is more than the parts, varies with the parts, and can reveal location

A group of pictured animals was shown on the flannel board. "Where are we?" was asked. A picture of an animal from a different habitat was added to the group, and the question was repeated. At the end of the series of additions, the class could answer only, "The Zoo!" A lion, tiger, and monkey formed the original group; then there appeared a giraffe, a camel, a polar bear, and finally a sea lion.

Illustrate the concept developed

The following list was shown:

> Building a fire to make irons red-hot
> Separating young animals from mothers
> Throwing animals on ground with hind feet tied
> Dragging animals toward fire
> Holding red-hot iron on left shoulder for ten seconds
> Making scar that will never go away

The class discussed the common element, what was being done, where the activity was going on, and whether the total was as cruel as the parts seemed.

The statement was formulated: "On ranches the branding of animals, which sounds cruel, furnishes necessary identification."

The class wrote the paragraph which developed this total statement.

ADDITIONAL TOPICS

> Details of crowded halls
> Details of crowded cafeteria
> Details of excitement at a game
> Details of activity in an auditorium just before a program
> Details of a scene at a fire
> Details of a crowded supermarket

LESSON III

Objective: Developing an understanding of generalization

Recall that the total is more than the parts

"WHAT DO ALL THESE ADD UP TO?"

> They make me go to bed early.
> Mother makes me wash the dishes alone.
> Father won't let me play ball with my friends.
> My older sister always sneaks the icing off my cake.
> My little brother ties knots in my shoelaces.

The class formed the total statement: "Everybody in our family picks on me."

Show how generalizations are formed

The teacher recalled the child who looked at a red sweater and said, "Hot!" because of having been warned away from a red-hot stove, red-hot fire, and red-hot toaster. The class decided that he had gone wrong because he had added up the wrong parts.

Show how generalizations state the total of the parts

From the following groups, the class selected the sentence most like "Everybody in our family picks on me."

Sue is a pleasant person.
She helps me study my English.
I've seen her running errands for her mother.
She has a gentle voice.
She smiles at my little brother.

Our picnic was a great success.
Each one of us ate three hamburgers.
Our team won the tug-of-war.
Mother had baked us a big chocolate cake.
The threatened rain didn't come.

There will be nearly 2,000 students.
The classes will eat lunch in a cafeteria.
We'll move to another room after each period.
Junior high school will be different from elementary school.
Teachers will be different for each subject.

When the students were asked how they selected the similar sentences, they decided that such sentences didn't give the parts but stated the total and that for every such sentence its parts must be stated.

Illustrate the concept

"This classroom is full" was recognized as a generalization that needed the support of a list of parts composing the total.

The class wrote the paragraph that gave the parts needed to support the generalization.

ADDITIONAL TOPICS

This school is different.
Our school is well equipped.
My duties at home keep me busy.
Looking after my little brother takes time.
Our new car has many accessories.

LESSON IV

Objective: Recognizing the function of a generalization

Locate a generalization and test its relation to the parts

In a student paragraph, the class found the generalization, tested whether the details would add up to support it or whether any detail was included that wouldn't, and noted whether the generalization appeared more than once.

In a textbook, the students found generalizations in some selected paragraphs, noted their position (usually at the beginning but sometimes at the end), determined that their function was to focus on a single idea, and decided that neither the parts nor the total could be omitted.

Use the generalization to test for relevancy of details

By examining the following lists, the class found that not all items in a list can be added and that irrelevant details must be removed:

4 pitchers, 3 catchers, 6 fielders, 2 shortstops, 1 referee
2 cows, 3 plows, 4 sows, 5 scows

The class examined the following paragraph.

> Cheryl enjoys sports. She likes to watch the Orioles on television, and sometimes as a special treat her father takes her to the Stadium to watch them play a home game. She looks forward to the City-Poly game at Thanksgiving, and she wouldn't miss that football match for anything. Her brother has taken her to watch some basketball games that she thought were very exciting. To her, lacrosse seems too fast and rough to be fun, even though in England it's considered a girls' game. Anybody can see that Cheryl is a real sports enthusiast.

They noted the two positions of the generalization, saw that it gave key words (*pleasure, sports*), and removed the one detail that proved irrelevant when tested against the key words.

Illustrate the concept

After finding the key words in the generalization, "Americans like many different kinds of sports," the class wrote a paragraph supporting it.

ADDITIONAL TOPICS

Television has many different kinds of programs.
Children have lots of irritating habits.
This room looks upset.
Loading a car requires careful planning.
Getting into condition involves many kinds of exercises.
Staying in condition means giving up many pleasures.
The moment before the whistle blows is exciting.

LESSON V

Objective: Developing the concept that sense perceptions can be the source of the concrete details necessary to support a generalization

Recognize that communication occurs through symbols that make a code

COMMUNICATION TAKES PLACE THROUGH NONVERBAL SYMBOLS

The function of the branding iron was recalled, and the significance of brands in making a code was discussed.

On the flannel board were shown common symbols: a figure of Uncle Sam; the hammer and sickle; the red, green, and yellow of a traffic light; the S-curve sign; the donkey and the elephant. Their significance in communicating was discussed.

A large-scale road map was displayed, and the communication significance of the color and type of lettering and of the size of markings
was discussed.

The class decided that the essential element of any symbol was a
common agreement on what it was supposed to represent and that
a symbol had meaning only to a person who was familiar with it.

*Recognize that because a symbol first becomes significant through
sense perceptions these are essential to communicating*

The class was asked what these things would add up to if they were
merely seen through a glass wall: chocolate cake, hamburger, potato
salad, lettuce and tomatoes, and rolls. After the class decided that they
formed a summer supper, it was asked to visualize burned edges on
the hamburger and ants on the potato salad. The class agreed that
their calling it a picnic came from only sight and their own experiences.

The class was asked to list the foods that a blindfolded person could
recognize by smell alone at a Thanksgiving dinner. Pupils offered
these: roast turkey, brussels sprouts, freshly baked rolls, sauerkraut,
and mince pie. They saw that smells can communicate to someone
who has had experience enough to know what the smells mean.

Then the class imagined a person with a cold in his head and sitting
blindfolded on a front porch, and it listed the sounds that would
tell him where he was, if he was familiar with them: the squeal of
tires, the sound of automobile horns, children's voices, a policeman's
whistle, and the wail of fire engine and ambulance sirens.

A volunteer was blindfolded and asked to identify objects by touch:
a bottle, pen, blotting paper, eraser, flower, wallet, bread, leather,
fabrics. If he failed to identify one by touch, the class would see
that sense perceptions give meaning to symbols only through experiences.

The class developed the idea that communication is possible through
sense perceptions but only when they have been experienced. It was
asked whether we would understand the smell of vinegar outside a
fish-and-chips shop and whether an Eskimo would recognize the smell
of pizza.

Illustrate the concept

The class was asked to imagine an English boy of their own age who
had never seen a watermelon and to determine what sense perceptions
a writer would have to give him if he was to understand the generalization shown: A favorite dessert is a well-chilled watermelon.

The class decided that it would be necessary to start on the outside
with color, shape, size. Going to the inside ("When it is cut" was
given) would require mentioning color, juice, seeds and a warning
against them, sound, and perhaps an explanation of the name.

The paragraph was written.

ADDITIONAL TOPICS

A description based on sense perceptions of
    A hot dog sandwich for an English boy
    A submarine sandwich for your grandmother

A barbecued beef sandwich for an Argentine boy
A soft crab sandwich for a Midwestern boy
Pizza for an Eskimo boy
An ear of corn for a Chinese boy
Lemon meringue pie for a Mexican boy

LESSON XII *

Objective: Developing an understanding of the difference between fact, inference, and judgment

*Recall how in the previous lesson clues were combined to determine
the tone established in the recordings*

Recognize the nature of inference

The following groups of statements were shown the class, which then
discussed the questions listed under each group::

1. On Friday Lindsay got the best report in the class.
2. On Saturday his father bought him a bicycle.

What might have happened in his family during the school term? Is
this conclusion a fact? Are the two statements facts? How is the
conclusion related to the two statements? Is it the only conclusion
possible?

1. Mother left a chocolate cake on the table.
2. Half an hour later, the icing was gone.
3. My little brother had chocolate on his mouth.

What is the inference? Is it the only inference possible?

1. Jack got the second test question wrong.
2. Jane sits next to Jack.
3. Jane got the second test question wrong.

What is the inference? Is it the only inference possible?

1. Robert had a party on his sixth birthday.
2. The present he was most excited about was a box of pencils
stamped with his name.

What month was Robert's birthday in? Is this the only inference
possible?

Distinguish between probable and less probable inferences

When a boy doesn't find a word in the dictionary, should he say "I
can't find the word" or "The word isn't there"?

When a boy can't find his book, should he say "I don't remember where
I left it" or "Somebody took it"?

*Recall the definition of report and fact, and distinguish inferences from
them*

---

* Lessons VI through XI are omitted from this article.

Illustrate the concept

The students wrote a paragraph describing an incident in the cafeteria through using facts and reports but no inferences.

ADDITIONAL TOPICS

Description of a quarrel, all facts and reports
Description of a person, all facts and reports
Description of a quarrel written by the person involved (including inferences) or by an impartial outsider (no inferences)
Description of an incident in class written by an impartial observer or written as if told at home

LESSON XIII

Objective: Developing an understanding of the difference between facts and judgments

Recognize the distinction between facts and judgments

A drawing of a snarling tiger and one of a purring cat were shown, and the class was asked which picture was more suitable for the following sentences:

Bill is a nice boy; I like him. But I hate Roger. He's no good.

The class decided that, because no facts had been given, these statements represented merely an emotion, interesting but not communicative.

The class was asked to select "snarl" and "purr" words from the following list: *lovely, sweet, awful, terrible, terrific.*

An anecdote was told of the boy who described his girl before and after she had broken a date with him, and the class was asked to select which of the following pairs of words he might use to describe her: *fat* and *plump, slender* and *skinny.*

The class was asked to decide whether the following paragraphs contain facts or judgments:

Everybody ought to subscribe to the school paper. It's a good paper, and I think the editor does a fine job. It helps school spirit, and everybody ought to read it. Buy the paper and boost, don't knock, our school!

There's one television program I like very much. I watch it whenever I can. It holds my interest, and I look forward to it every week. Many people say they like it too. Why don't you try it sometime? You'll enjoy it also, I'm sure.

The class concluded that judgments expressed only in "snarl" and "purr" words are useless and that judgments must be supported by reports and facts.

Illustrate the difference

The class wrote a recommendation for a TV program (a book, a hobby, a game, a candidate), making sure that facts supporting the judgments were given and that mere "purr" words were avoided.

SEVENTH-GRADE PARAGRAPHS
DEVELOPED IN THE LESSONS[2]

Supporting a Generalization

This class room is full. There are about 40 spectators. There is room for only one or two more people. There are 48 students. There is not much room between rows. There are two large screens, two large projectors, and a tape recorder. We have as many desks as pupils. We even have two book racks. There is also a microphone. We have a locker behind one door and three double lockers behind the other. There is extra space for our teacher, Dr. Graser.

Developing a Generalization from Key Words

Americans enjoy many different kinds of sports. We have many sports in different groups that Americans enjoy. For example, football, baseball, basketball, softball, and hockey are team sports. Boxing and wrestling are sports against a single opponent. Horse racing, skiing, boat racing, and water skiing are individual sports. All of these are sports that Americans enjoy.

Sense Perceptions as a Source of Detail

A favorite dessert is a chilled watermelon. On the outside it's the color of a cucumber, light green and dark green. A watermelon is about fourteen inches long and about six and a half inches wide. The watermelon has an oval or huge egg shape. When it's cut the inside is red with some white, brown and black seeds, and it's filled with juice. As you eat it, it sounds like it's crunching to you but other people can't hear anything. From this information you should know that "It's a pure delight."

Reports as a Source of Detail

My uncle says a Volkswagen is a good buy. That is, it gives good transportation for a low cost. The Volkswagen is under $2000. It gives long mileage. That is, it gives long riding for little gas—25 miles to a gallon. It's easy parking in the city

---

[2] Because time was limited, the students had almost no opportunity to revise their work, each paper having been written in about one quarter-hour. Therefore, the students agreed to let the teacher correct spelling and punctuation and make slight changes in phrasing. All such changes are underlined.

because it takes such little space. My uncle thinks a Volkswagen is worth more than its cost.

Arrangements in Space

As I sit here, I can see many things on the top of my desk. Moving clockwise, I can see the pen that I write with and my name plate. I can also see my folder that is a light yellow and is made of cardboard. On top of it is a notebook of white and black with my name and grade on it, made of heavy cardboard. In the middle of my desk is a long yellow pad, with many sheets of paper on it, and on top of it is a wooden pencil and at the end of it is lead. On the yellow pad is a lot of words that are talking about what's on my desk. On the whole desk is heavy green paper and on the heavy green paper is a picture of a horse and a heart with S. W. on it, and tape.

As I sit here, moving clockwise I can see many things on the top of my desk. I can see a name plate, a set of eight new magic markers which in color are orange, black, blue, brown, red, green, yellow, and purple. I see two arms writing with a pencil on a pad. I also see a Schooltime Composition book with my name, the school I go to, and the grade with white paper between two pieces of cardboard and a folder with yellow and white paper in it. In the name plate I see the ball point of a pen and underneath it all is a big piece of green paper.

Supporting a Generalization by an Incident

I've found that sounds can be pleasant. On a farm where I visit I helped around with the animals, mostly the sheep and the chickens. And at the end of the day when the animals were bedded down, it was a nice calm sound but it was not still. You could hear the cattle but it was calm. Then I went to bed and heard the crickets outside. But when I woke up I heard somebody putting the griddle for hot cakes on the stove. The sounds of a farm are all pleasant.

Providing Fullness of Detail

To come here on Monday you must come out of the front door and turn right, go up to Charlton Road, and go right. At the corner of Charlton go up to Kilburn, then on to the Esso Station straight up the street. Wait for the 28 bus and get off at Liberty Heights. Walk across Liberty Heights and go straight about 2 or 3 blocks. When you get to the school go in the front door and go up a little way and turn left to the first room and you are there.

The scope of the concepts these students approached in the above lessons is broad. It can embrace work with the English code for communication, work with consistency of approach to the reader and elimination of ambiguity, work with exact and vivid diction, and work with the affective devices of rhetoric. The concepts relate to college freshmen as well as to seventh graders. Even the approaches to the concepts that these lessons present are versatile. Because these three concepts are basic, students who approach them again and again, each time in greater depth, should grasp them with increased understanding. As illustrations of how the concept of transmitting the message might be reapproached at different and deeper levels, lessons designed for a brief unit with eighth-, tenth-, and eleventh-grade average students have been added to those used in the three-week seventh-grade sessions.

Three weeks is a very short time. Yet the above samples of their writing showed that after three weeks of study during a hot Baltimore July, a group of seventh-grade volunteers began to grasp the three fundamental concepts of composition. Isn't it likely that as these youngsters study these principles more deeply and more often, eventually they will comprehend the structure of communication, that is, see how the parts are related to the whole? Perhaps they will begin also to see themselves as parts in the whole of society.

11

Grading and Measuring

Paul B. Diederich
Director of Research in English
*Educational Testing Service**

COLLEGE BOARD EXPERIENCE

The College Entrance Examination Board used nothing but essay examinations from 1900 to 1926, then used a mixture of essays and objective tests, and since 1941 has used chiefly objective tests. Although the latter yielded better predictions of academic success, and although their wide sampling of content gave teachers greater freedom, there was continual pressure to return to the essay in at least one examination. Several costly

* Paul B. Diederich took his B.A. and M.A. degrees at Harvard, and his Ph.D. at Columbia. He taught in private and public high schools from 1930 to 1940 and was associate professor of English and examiner in English for the United States Armed Forces Institute at the University of Chicago from 1940 to 1950. Dr. Diederich has been a member of the Research Division of Educational Testing Service in Princeton, New Jersey, since that time and is known chiefly for the experimental tryout of the use of readers to assist high school English teachers in grading and correcting compositions. With Osmond E. Palmer he is author of a book of instructional tests for college freshmen, *Critical Thinking in Reading and Writing* (Holt, 1955). His article "The Rutgers Plan for Cutting Class Size in Two" appeared in *The English Journal* in April 1960.

experiments were conducted using essays up to two hours in length, each graded by two or more College Board readers. But these readers did not agree very closely on the merit of the papers, and the students were even more erratic. The quality of their writing varied a great deal from one occasion or topic to another. As a result, final grades on two long essays agreed only 0.45 with one another, whereas scores on two objective tests of verbal ability, taken at the time of writing the essays, agreed 0.88.

It became obvious that further progress could be made only by finding out what qualities in student writing affect readers differently, causing a difference in their grading. It seemed unlikely that capable readers would disagree so wildly unless they were looking at different things or weighting them differently.

MATERIALS FOR A STUDY OF READER REACTIONS

To study this question, the writer and two colleagues [1] in the Research Division of Educational Testing Service secured 600 papers written as homework between one class meeting and the next by freshmen at Cornell, Middlebury, and the University of Pennsylvania. There were four topics, but only two were chosen by enough students: "Who Should Go to College?" and "When Should Teenagers Be Treated as Adults?" They were told that their papers would be read by 60 distinguished readers in six different fields: college English teachers, social science teachers, natural science teachers, writers and editors, lawyers, and business executives. The students were more stimulated than frightened by such an audience because they knew that their papers would be typed and reproduced without identification and that grades would not be reported to anyone.

We reduced the 600 papers to 300 (150 on each topic) without reading them: first, by dropping papers on the two less popular topics; second, by looking at the Scholastic Aptitude Test verbal scores of the writers. Since we wanted as wide a range as possible, we kept all papers written by students with either high or low SAT verbal scores and reduced the number

---

[1] Diederich, Paul B.; French, John W.; and Carlton, Sydell T. *Factors in Judgments of Writing Ability.* Research Bulletin 61-15. Princeton, N. J.: Educational Testing Service, 1961. (Out of print.)

with middle scores in such fashion that the distribution of verbal ability on one topic was parallel to that on the other. The remaining papers on both topics represented a wider range in verbal ability than any one teacher would be likely to encounter in a selective college. It may be said at once that we found no significant difference of any kind between one topic and the other. Hence our conclusions can be generalized at least to the types of short expository papers that are commonly assigned in both high schools and colleges.

HOW THE PAPERS WERE GRADED

The readers were told to sort the papers into nine piles in order of general merit. No instructions were given as to what to look for, since we wanted to find out what the readers looked for when they were free to grade as they liked. The only rules were that all nine piles must be used, and not less than six papers on each topic must appear in the smallest piles. The readers were also asked to comment on anything they liked or disliked in as many papers as possible.

The result was nearly chaos. Of the 300 papers, 101 received all nine grades, 111 received eight, 70 received seven, and no paper received less than five. The average agreement (correlation) among all readers was 0.31; among the college English teachers, 0.41. Readers in the other five fields agreed with the English teachers slightly better than they agreed with other readers in their own field.

This procedure has been criticized on the ground that we could have secured a higher level of agreement had we defined each topic more precisely, used only English teachers as readers, and spent some time in coming to agreements upon common standards. So we could, but then we would have found only the qualities we agreed to look for—possibly with a few surprises. We wanted each reader to go his own way so that differences in grading standards would come to light. We used readers in five fields in addition to English teachers because our colleagues also have opinions on the writing ability of our students, and so do representatives of the educated public.

THE FACTOR ANALYSIS

We correlated the grades of each reader with the grades of every other reader and put this large table of agreements and disagreements through the mathematical procedure known as "factor analysis." This is too complicated to explain briefly, but the effect is as though the computer scanned all the correlations and picked out clusters of readers who agreed with one another and disagreed with other clusters to a greater degree than could come about by chance. There proved to be only five such clusters. They were clearly agreeing on something, and on something different in each cluster. What was it?

We found out by tabulating the comments of the three readers who stood highest on each factor (who came closest to the central tendency of each cluster) and only on papers graded either high (7-8-9) or low (1-2-3). We checked our conclusions by similarly tabulating the comments of the three readers who stood lowest on each factor. Comments were tabulated under 55 headings by a person who did not know the standing of any reader on any factor. In all, 11,018 comments on 3,557 papers were tabulated. They were reduced to percentages of total comments written by each reader so that readers who wrote the most comments would not unduly influence the interpretation.

It then became quite clear that the largest cluster (16 readers) was influenced primarily by the *ideas* expressed: their richness, soundness, clarity, development, and relevance. The next largest (13 readers) was most influenced by *mechanics*: the number of errors in grammar or usage, punctuation, and spelling. Seven of the ten English teachers stood high on this factor. The third (9 readers) showed the highest interest in *organization* and analysis. Four of the business executives stood high on this factor. (They were also especially sensitive to poor spelling but not to other elements of mechanics.) The fourth (9 readers) stood highest in specific comments on *wording* and phrasing: on verbal felicity or infelicity. The fifth (7 readers) emphasized style, individuality, interest, sincerity, the personal qualities of the writing, which we decided to call *flavor*. The four readers who stood highest on this factor were all writers or editors. They also had the lowest percentage of specific comments on mechanical errors.

Here, evidently, were some of the reasons why expert College Board readers had so long failed to agree. Like the distinguished readers assembled for this study, they were responding to different qualities in the papers, or they differed in the weights they attached to these qualities. One possible conclusion might be that papers in important tests of writing ability should be rated by five different readers, each of whom was especially sensitive to one of these factors. Since this was hardly feasible, it was comforting to find no solid evidence that any reader was entirely blind to any of these qualities. There were only differences in emphasis, heightened by the absence of directives and amplified by the technique of factor analysis. If readers were asked for a rating on each factor or on some of its principal components, it seemed likely that all but a few readers would be able to follow these instructions.

This policy was tried out in three large high schools the following year. The principal new finding was that, under the pressure of time and the teaching tradition, these five factors collapsed into two: a general merit factor and a distinct mechanics factor. The ratings that had the highest "loadings" on the general merit factor were, however, four of our five original factors: ideas, organization, flavor, and wording. While we might have settled for a single rating on merit and another on mechanics, we decided to ask for a separate rating on the four main components of each in order to make the totals more reliable. Since we were now dealing with handwritten papers, the mechanics factor was broadened to include a rating on handwriting and neatness as well as on grammar and sentence structure, punctuation, and spelling.

DEFINITION OF POINTS ON THE RATING SCALE

During the past year, English departments in 17 high schools have rated monthly test papers written in class for these eight qualities, each on a scale of 1 (low) to 5 (high). For the benefit of students, high, middle, and low points on each quality were defined in very simple terms, as follows:

General Merit

1. Ideas

High. The student has given some thought to the topic and has written what he really thinks. He discusses each main point long enough to show clearly what he means. He supports each main point with arguments, examples, or details; he gives the reader some reason for believing it. His points are clearly related to the topic and to the main idea or impression he is trying to get across. No necessary points are overlooked and there is no padding.

Middle. The paper gives the impression that the student does not really believe what he is writing or does not fully realize what it means. He tries to guess what the teacher wants and writes what he thinks will get by. He does not explain his points very clearly or make them come alive to the reader. He writes what he thinks will sound good, not what he believes or knows.

Low. It is either hard to tell what points the student is trying to make or else they are so silly that he would have realized that they made no sense if he had only stopped to think. He is only trying to get something down on paper. He does not explain his points; he only writes them and then goes on to something else, or he repeats them in slightly different words. He does not bother to check his facts, and much of what he writes is obviously untrue. No one believes this sort of writing—not even the student who wrote it.

2. Organization

High. The paper starts at a good point, moves in a straight line, gets somewhere, and stops at a good point. The paper has a plan that the reader can follow; he is never in doubt as to where he is or where he is going. Sometimes there is a little twist near the end that makes the paper come out in a way that the reader does not expect, but it seems quite logical. Main points are treated at greatest length or with greatest emphasis; others, in proportion to their importance.

Middle. The organization of this paper is standardized and conventional. There is usually a one-paragraph introduction, then three main points each treated in one paragraph, and then a conclusion, which often seems tacked on or forced. Some trivial points may be treated in greater detail than important points, and there is usually some dead wood that might better be cut out.

Low. This paper starts anywhere and never gets anywhere. The main points are not clearly separated from one another, and they come in a random order—as though the student had not given any thought to what he intended to say before he sat down to write. The paper seems to start in one direction, then another, then another, until the reader is lost.

3. Flavor

High. The writing sounds like a person, not a committee. The writer seems quite sincere and candid, and he writes about something he knows—often from personal experience. You could never mistake this writing for the writing of anyone else. Although the writer may play different roles in different papers, he does not put on airs. He is brave enough to reveal himself just as he is.

Middle. The writer usually tries to appear better or wiser than he really is. He tends to write lofty sentiments and broad generalities. He does not put in the little, homely details that show that he knows what he is talking about. His writing tries to sound impressive. Sometimes it is impersonal and correct but colorless, without personal feeling or imagination.

Low. The writer reveals himself well enough but without meaning to. His thoughts and feelings are those of an uneducated person who does not realize how bad they sound. His way of expressing himself differs from standard English, but it is not his personal style; it is the way uneducated people talk in his neighborhood.

4. Wording

High. The writer uses a sprinkling of uncommon words or of familiar words in an uncommon setting. He shows an interest in words and in putting them together in slightly unusual ways. Some of his experiments with words may not quite come off, but this is such a promising trait in a young writer that a few mistakes may be forgiven. For the most part he uses words correctly, but he also uses them with imagination.

Middle. The writer is addicted to tired old phrases and hackneyed expressions. If you left a blank in one of his sentences, almost anyone could guess what word he would use at that point. He does not stop to think how to say something; he just says it in the same way as everyone else. A writer may also get a middle rating on this quality if he overdoes his experiments with uncommon words: if he always uses a big word when a little word would serve his purpose better.

Low. The writer uses words so carelessly or inexactly that he gets far too many wrong. These are not intentional experiments with words in which failure may be forgiven; they represent groping for words and using them without regard to their fitness. A paper written entirely in a childish vocabulary may also get a low rating, even if no word is clearly wrong.

Mechanics

5. Grammar, Sentence Structure

High. There are no vulgar or "illiterate" errors in grammar or usage by present standards of informal written English, and there are very few errors in points that have been emphasized in class. The sentence structure is usually correct, even in varied and complicated sentence patterns.

Middle. There are a few serious errors in grammar and several in points that have been emphasized in class, but not enough to obscure meaning. The sentence structure is usually correct in the more familiar sentence patterns, but there are occasional errors in more complicated patterns such as parallelism, subordination, consistency of tenses, reference of pronouns, etc.

Low. There are so many serious errors in grammar and sentence structure that the paper is hard to understand.

6. Punctuation

High. There are no serious violations of rules that have been taught—except slips of the pen. Note, however, that modern editors do not require commas after short introductory phrases, around nonrestrictive clauses, or between short coordinate clauses unless their omission leads to ambiguity or makes the sentence hard to read.

Middle. There are several violations of rules that have been taught—as many as usually occur in the average paper.

Low. Basic punctuation is omitted or haphazard, resulting in fragments, run-on sentences, etc.

7. Spelling

High. Since this rating scale is most often used for test papers written in class, when there is insufficient time to use the dictionary, spelling standards should be more lenient than for papers written at home. The high paper usually has not more than five misspellings, and these occur in words that are hard to spell. The spelling is consistent: words are not spelled correctly in one sentence and misspelled in another, unless the misspelling appears to be a slip of the pen. If a poor paper has no misspellings, it gets a 5 in spelling.

Middle. There are several spelling errors in hard words and a few violations of basic spelling rules, but no more than one finds in the average paper.

Low. There are so many spelling errors that they interfere with comprehension.

8. Handwriting, Neatness

High. The handwriting is clear, attractive, and well spaced, and the rules of manuscript form have been observed.

Middle. The handwriting is average in legibility and attractiveness. There may be a few violations of rules for manuscript form if there is evidence of some care for the appearance of the page.

Low. The paper is sloppy in appearance and difficult to read.

THE MEASUREMENT OF GROWTH IN WRITING ABILITY

The only scientific way known to the writer to measure growth in writing ability by means of essays is to have all students in a span of three grades write a paper on the same topic and on the same day, at least four times a year and preferably six or eight. To keep nervous teachers from coaching students on the topic set for each date, the department may first agree on a long list of topics as suitable for short, impromptu compositions to be written in class. Then, at the beginning of each testing day, the department head may simply announce, "Today we'll use Topic 7," or "Today we'll use Topic 18." All English teachers write this topic on their blackboards, read aloud any explanatory material that accompanies it, and devote that day to the writing of test essays. Students number their own papers with any number of six digits that pops into their heads, such as 924,332 or 001,644, and they write no other identification on their papers. They copy this number on a 3 x 5 index card and add their name, grade, curriculum, other designations such as "regular" or "honors," and their teacher's name. These cards are locked up by the principal until the grading is finished.

The papers are distributed in a random fashion to all members of the department and rated on the scale previously discussed, without knowledge of the identity of the writers or their grade, curriculum, or teacher. In experimental studies, these ratings are usually recorded on separate 3 x 5 cards and no comments or corrections are written on the papers, so as not to influence the ratings of a second reader. For ordinary school use, however, each student may be asked to write a column of numbers from 1 to 8 in the upper left-hand corner of his first page. These numbers refer to the eight qualities defined in the rating scale, and the teacher who first gets the paper records his ratings on a scale of 1 (low) to 5 (high) opposite each of these eight numbers. When the paper is returned to this student's English teacher, he rates the paper again and records his ratings to the right of those already recorded by the first reader. He then adds together both sets of ratings to get a total rating for that paper, which may range from 16 (low) through 48 (average) to 80 (high). After four test papers, the cumulative total ratings may range from 64 to 320.

At the end of each period on testing days, when students hand in their papers, their teacher sorts the papers into as many piles as there are teachers and/or readers to read them. If there are eight, he sorts the papers into eight piles. At the end of the testing day, he cross-stacks these piles and takes them to the room of the department head, who has eight chairs lined up to receive them. Each teacher drops one pile of his papers on each chair until each chair holds a random eighth of the papers written in each English class that day. Each teacher or reader picks up his eighth and rates the papers at home. After a little practice, most teachers learn to rate these short test papers in about two minutes per paper if they do not write in corrections. They may, however, write a brief comment on anything they like or dislike.

Teachers often complain that they do not know how to rate a paper if they do not know whether it comes from the tenth or twelfth grade or from regular or honors classes. They hold up a paper and say that it should get a 4 in some quality if it comes from a regular class but only 2 or 3 if it comes from an honors class. There are many replies to this objection, but the most devastating is that, if they had this knowledge, the effect would be precisely the opposite. Benjamin Rosner of Brooklyn College added such bits of information to otherwise anonymous papers to see what the effect would be; what the readers did not know was that half of his information was true and half was false. Papers labeled "boy" received the same average grades as when they were labeled "girl," but papers labeled "honors" received average grades that were significantly higher than when these same papers were labeled "regular." This deception was tried out on so many teachers in different schools that there is no doubt that this tendency is general. We find what we expect to find. If we think a paper was written by an honors student, it looks better than if we think it was written by a regular student.

Anyway, all that the rating yields is a series of numbers representing total ratings on each paper. These numbers can then be adjusted for grade and curriculum before being translated into grades that will stand in the record. One simply makes a distribution of these totals for each curriculum within each grade. Then, if it has been decided that the tenth-grade regular students include (let us say) 20 students who ought to get A's, one counts 20 ratings down from the top for that group, draws a line, and calls everything above it an A. The 20 students who stand above this line may not be the same 20 who "ought" to get A's (and who *will* get A's on the other bases that were used in coming to this decision), but at least this procedure assures the desired proportions of letter grades for each group. No one gets a D simply because he is a tenth-grade vocational student who cannot yet meet the competition of higher grades and harder curriculums. If he stands high among his own group, he gets a high grade, no matter where his total rating falls in the distribution for the entire school.

This latter distribution, however, will show him where he stands in relation to the entire student body and how his standing changes from one year to the next. In grade 10, the average student stands in the lowest third of this distribution; in grade 11, in the middle third; in grade 12, in the top third; and in all grades the academic students tend to stand far above the non-academic. This is a realistic view of one's competition, and it is the only scientific way thus far developed to measure the amount of improvement in writing from one year to the next. The idea that teachers can judge the amount of growth by the old process of marking papers severely at the beginning of a year and leniently at the end is utter nonsense that ought not to deceive a child. It does, but it is a deception that should not be practiced on the young. Growth can be plotted only when each test paper is judged against a background of a representative sample of papers from the entire school, and only when the teachers do not know which papers are which. Then, if a student accumulates 128 points in his first year, 192 in his second, and 256 in his third, the rise in his standing is meaningful.

THEME GRADING

Ordinary grading of homework assignments in composition cannot make use of the rigorous departmental procedures we have recommended for test essays. On the whole, it is better not to attempt anything of the sort, since anonymity works better in testing than in instruction. One of John McNulty's sketches is charmingly entitled "A Man Like Grady, You Got To Know Him First." To help a student, you also have to know him first. It remains to be seen, however, whether it is wise or appropriate to grade these homework assignments at all, so long as the test essays are there to give the student his bearings. Many teachers prefer to give their reactions and suggestions entirely by written or spoken comments. Others like to use the rating scale, but only as an estimate of probable ratings had this been a test essay, not as marks that stand in the record. This appears to be a matter of preference. One must only remember that the homework assignments reveal problems that have no numerical solutions. It would be unfortunate if ratings on these papers were mistaken for answers and thereby headed off any real effort to find answers.

Appendixes

Appendix A:

Criteria for Use in Grading and Revising Themes

POINTS TO CONSIDER IN CORRECTING THEMES

Prepared by Arno Jewett

1. *Purpose*
   a. How clearly is the purpose or thesis stated?
   b. How well is it achieved?
   c. Is the topic sufficiently limited?

2. *Content*
   a. Are the main ideas evident to the reader?
   b. Are details given to develop main ideas or topics?
   c. Are examples used to illustrate and support general statements?
   d. Is the content related to the writer's purpose?
   e. Are facts or evidence accurate or verifiable?

3. *Organization* (Unity)
   a. Does the introduction prepare the reader for what follows?
   b. Is there a clear relationship among main ideas?
   c. Are transitions from one idea or topic to another clearly made?
   d. Does the theme have a definite, satisfactory conclusion?

4. *Style* (Flavor)
   a. Is sentence structure varied and smooth?
   b. Is diction vivid and suitable?
   c. Is figurative language fresh and fitting?
   d. Is the tone appropriate to purpose and subject?
   e. Does the theme hold the reader's attention?
5. *Mechanics*
   a. Have the conventions of grammar and usage been observed?
   b. Is correct punctuation used to aid the reader?
   c. Are words spelled correctly?

Note: If the errors in mechanics detract from the readability and content of the paper, give a split grade, the lower grade for mechanics.

A SCALE FOR GRADING ENGLISH COMPOSITION

Developed by Paul B. Diederich,
Director of Research in English, Educational Testing Service,
and recommended by the
NEA-Dean Langmuir Project on English Composition

1-Poor 2-Weak 3-Avg.	4-Good	5-Excellent	Reader_____
Quality and development of ideas	1 2 3 4 5		
Organization, relevance, movement	1 2 3 4 5	_____ × 5 = _____ Subtotal	
Style, flavor, individuality	1 2 3 4 5		
Wording and phrasing	1 2 3 4 5	_____ × 3 = _____ Subtotal	
Grammar, sentence structure	1 2 3 4 5		
Punctuation	1 2 3 4 5		
Spelling	1 2 3 4 5		
Manuscript form, legibility	1 2 3 4 5	_____ × 1 = _____ Subtotal	
		Total grade _____%	

How To Interpret This Scale

1. This scale weighs content and organization 50 percent, aspects of style 30 percent, and mechanics 20 percent. The multiplication translates the 40-point scale into a 100-point scale.

2. The ratings for each item range from 1 to 5. Regard 1 as the lowest grade, 3 as the average, and 5 as the highest. Use 2 to designate below-average performance but not marked deficiency, and use 4 to designate above-average performance but not marked proficiency. Reading 5 randomly selected papers from a set before you attempt to grade the set will help you to form a realistic notion of 1, 3, and 5 performance for that particular assignment.

3. Observing the following guidelines will also help to ensure more uniform and consistent grading.

   a. *Quality and development of ideas.* Grant the writer his choice of subject matter. He was, after all, offered choices dictated by the teacher and should *not* be penalized by the value you place on one choice as compared to another. Look for how well he has supported his subject and *his* point of view or attitude toward the subject.

   b. *Organization, relevance, movement.* A 5 paper will begin with a clear indication of its controlling idea, offer convincing relevant support, and come to a close. A 1 paper begins anywhere and goes nowhere. A 3 paper may be skimpily but relevantly developed or fully developed but include some irrelevant material.

   c. *Style, flavor, individuality.* Guard against the temptation to give a low score for the use of substandard English. Papers containing substandard English are often rich in flavor and individuality. Reserve 5 for the truly arresting paper. A single apt, precise, or arresting phrase can move a paper from a 3 to a 4.

   d. *Wording and phrasing.* Here is the place to give a low score for an impoverished vocabulary and a high one for apt and precise diction and clear phrasing.

   e. *Grammar, sentence structure.* Low scores should be given for frequent *and varied* substandard constructions like errors in agreement between subject and verb, in person or tense, faulty reference, and errors in agreement between pronoun and antecedent, dangling constructions.

   f. *Punctuation.* Again, frequent *and varied* abuses of standard punctuation marks deserve a low score; occasional varied errors in common punctuation marks, a middle score; freedom from common errors, a high score. Errors in the use of the comma, the apostrophe, and end punctuation should be regarded as more serious than errors in the use of the semicolon, quotation marks (especially double quotes), parentheses, and brackets. Regard the mistaken presence or absence of the apostrophe as a punctuation error, not a spelling error.

   g. *Spelling.* Give a score of 5 if the writer has misspelled no words; a 4 for one spelling error; a 3 for two spelling errors; a 2 for three spelling errors; and a 1 for four or more errors. This is the *only* place on the scale where you are to assess spelling. Misspelling the same word several times is only one error.

   h. *Manuscript form, legibility.* Adherence to manuscript form and a clearly readable paper merits a 5. An unreadable paper without margins and without a proper heading merits a score of 1. Perhaps readers should attempt only a 1, 3, or 5 judgment on this item. Do *not* give a low score for neat cross-outs. (Remember that the students are writing their Project papers in class and that they have been encouraged not to waste time recopying.)

DIRECTIONS TO STUDENTS
FOR REVISING PAPERS

1. Supply yourself with a dictionary, grammar rule book, spelling sheet, and error sheet. (The last two are available from the instructor.)

2. Review your paper carefully, and consider each symbol, comment, or question. In the right-hand margin, number each item marked by a symbol, comment, or question.

3. Use a separate sheet of paper for each page of your theme on which errors occur. Number your revision pages to correspond to the pages of the paper you are revising.

4. In line with EACH item to be revised, write its number and the revision. Write out only enough to make your revision clear and complete.

   Note: After each error in punctuation, write out the reason for your revision.

   Example: . . . and Jones, the lawyer, . . . (Use commas to set off an appositive)

5. In addition to correcting misspelled words on your revision pages, record the *correct* spelling of words you missed on your spelling sheet.

6. Record the number of each error you made on your error sheet.

7. Discard preliminary work returned to you.

8. Clip together, in the following order, your paper, the revisions, the spelling sheet, and the error sheet.

Note: Revisions are due at the beginning of the class period following the day the paper was returned to you.

Careful revision is the best single way to eliminate from your writing habits those errors in form and mechanics which mar your expression and prevent you from concentrating on the really important matter of what you want to say.

For this reason, no paper will be considered complete or entered for credit which has not been meticulously revised.

Remember, the best way to cut down revisions is to avoid repeating errors you made in previous papers. Before you prepare your final copy of any paper, you should go over the list of errors you made in the past and check your new paper for those errors. Generally speaking, you should check your paper for only one error at a time, even though this may require three or four rereadings. Five to fifteen minutes spent in pre-vision can save you an hour of revision; consistently practiced, this procedure can also cut down greatly in the total time you spend in writing a paper.

MARKING OF 250-WORD THEMES
Developed by Leonard Freyman
Based on data from the California Council of Teachers of English

Average Minutes per Theme

Minutes

3.5	Punctuation, spelling and placing grade on paper
5.9	All errors and placing grade with *no* explanation of errors
8.6	All errors, indicating *how* to correct, and noting favorable aspects for motivation

Hours by Pupil Load

Pupils

Hours

		0	5	10	15	20	25
100	Punctuation, spelling, grade		6				
	All errors and grade			10			
	All—with comments				15		
125	Punctuation, spelling, grade		7.5				
	All errors and grade			12.5			
	All—with comments					18.5	
150	Punctuation, spelling, grade			9			
	All errors and grade			15			
	All—with comments						22.5

Appendix B:

Guidelines for Participants
in a Theme Reader Program

by Leonard Freyman

The Theme Reader should—

1. Have ease of exchange, pickup, and delivery of papers.
2. Grade papers in the order in which they are received (unless priority is indicated) and assure prompt return of papers.
3. Understand the philosophy of the teacher; be able to judge relative values and sense of importance.
4. Have duplicate copies of all materials which students and teacher use in composition lab.
5. Have duplicate copies of supplementary materials to settle "fine points."
6. Write as many comments as possible on students' papers, stapling separate comment sheets on major papers.
7. Suggest additional books, poems, articles, etc., which will enlarge students' understanding.
8. Work out some sort of grade sheet or error sheet which will indicate persistent low-level achievement of a student; suggest that the teacher give special attention in whatever area is indicated.
9. Prepare a general comment sheet for each set of papers, noting over-all quality of papers in regard to content, originality, clarity,

etc., and calling attention to common errors in a given field—misplaced modifiers, illogical comparisons, faulty reference of pronouns, etc.

10. When there is doubt about the assigned grade, indicate your doubt on the grade sheet, giving the teacher an opportunity to double-check the grade in question.
11. Visit labs on request of the teacher.
12. Be seen. Students are curious as to what "the reader" looks like.
13. Have free access to the teacher's files to make periodic checks on student achievement.
14. Know as far in advance as possible when papers will be due. How many? What kind? Particularly, what length?

The Teacher should—

1. Make as clear assignments as possible.
2. Vary assignments when possible: i.e., if three classes are doing poetry analyses, choose three different poems.
3. Furnish an even flow of papers to the reader, staggering long papers when coming from a large group.
4. Always assume final authority for all grades.
5. Ask the reader for suggested composition assignments.
6. Ask the reader to advise when revisions are indicated.
7. Furnish the reader source materials on which compositions are based.
8. Inform the reader what length of time the students had in which to write a composition: i.e., one class period, a two-hour lab, overnight.

The Director should—

1. Schedule a conference with each reader at some time during the school year to—
   (a) discuss her experiences as a reader; her problems (if any).
   (b) acquaint the reader with her role as it relates to the over-all language arts program.
2. Set up a workshop during the school year where exhibits by teacher and lay reader at each grade level can be shared with fellow teachers and lay readers. Such a workshop would be informative and stimulating to everyone participating in the program; it would be a means of disseminating the best methods and practices which individual teachers and lay readers have perfected and found helpful.

Appendix C:
Bibliographies

FOR YOUR PROFESSIONAL LIBRARY

Composition and Rhetoric

BRADDOCK, RICHARD; LLOYD-JONES, RICHARD; and SCHOER, LOWELL. *Research in Written Composition.* Champaign, Ill.: National Council of Teachers of English, 1963.

BROWN, ROLLO WALTER. *How the French Boy Learns To Write.* Cambridge, Mass.: Harvard University Press, 1915; Champaign, Ill.: National Council of Teachers of English, 1963.

GUTH, HANS P. *English Today and Tomorrow, A Guide for Teachers of English.* Englewood Cliffs, N.J.: Prentice-Hall, 1964.

KITZHABER, ALBERT R. *Themes, Theories, and Therapy: The Teaching of Writing in College.* New York: McGraw-Hill Book Co., 1963.

Language

ALLEN, HAROLD B., editor. *Readings in Applied Linguistics.* Second edition. New York: Appleton-Century-Crofts, 1964.

BACH, EMMON. *An Introduction to Transformational Grammars.* New York: Holt, Rinehart and Winston, 1964.

DEAN, LEONARD F., and WILSON, KENNETH G., editors. *Essays on Language and Usage.* Second edition. New York: Oxford University Press, 1963.

FRANCIS, W. NELSON. *The Structure of American English.* New York: Ronald Press Co., 1958.

GLEASON, H. A. *An Introduction to Descriptive Linguistics.* Revised edition. New York: Holt, Rinehart and Winston, 1961.

JEWETT, ARNO; MERSAND, JOSEPH; and GUNDERSON, DORIS V., editors. *Improving English Skills of Culturally Different Youth in Large Cities.* U.S. Office of Health, Education, and Welfare, Office of Education, Bulletin 1964, No. 5. Washington, D.C.: Government Printing Office, 1964.

LAIRD, CHARLTON M., and GORRELL, ROBERT M., editors. *English as Language: Backgrounds, Development, Usage.* New York: Harcourt, Brace and World, 1961.

BIBLIOGRAPHY ON LANGUAGE AND LINGUISTICS

Adapted from basic list prepared by Kenneth G. Wilson

BAUGH, ALBERT C. *A History of the English Language.* Second edition. New York: Appleton-Century-Crofts, 1957.

BLOOMFIELD, LEONARD. *Language.* New York: Holt, Rinehart and Winston, 1933.

BRYANT, MARGARET. *Current American Usage.* New York: Funk & Wagnalls Co., 1962.

CARROLL, JOHN B. *The Study of Language: A Survey of Linguistics and Related Disciplines in America.* Cambridge, Mass.: Harvard University Press, 1953.

CHOMSKY, NOAM. *Syntactic Structures.* New York: Gregory Lounz, Books, 1957.

FRANCIS, W. NELSON. *The Structure of American English.* New York: Ronald Press Co., 1958.

FRIES, CHARLES CARPENTER. *American English Grammar.* New York: Appleton-Century-Crofts, 1940.

FRIES, CHARLES CARPENTER. *The Structure of English.* New York: Harcourt, Brace and World, 1952.

GLEASON, H. A., JR. *An Introduction to Descriptive Linguistics.* Second edition. New York: Holt, Rinehart and Winston, 1961.

HILL, A. A. *Introduction to Linguistic Structures: From Sound to Sentence in English.* New York: Harcourt, Brace and World, 1958.

HOIJER, HARRY, editor. *Language in Culture.* Chicago: University of Chicago Press, 1954.

JESPERSEN, J. O. H. *Essentials of English Grammar.* New York: Holt, Rinehart and Winston, 1933; University: University of Alabama Press, 1964.

LADO, ROBERT. *Linguistics Across Cultures.* Ann Arbor: University of Michigan Press, 1957.

LEHMANN, WINFRED P. *Historical Linguistics: An Introduction.* New York: Holt, Rinehart and Winston, 1962.

LLOYD, DONALD J., and WARFEL, HARRY R. *American English in Its Cultural Setting.* New York: Alfred A. Knopf, 1956.

MARCKWARDT, ALBERT H. *American English.* New York: Oxford University Press, 1958.

PEI, MARIO. *The Story of English.* New York: J. B. Lippincott Co., 1952.

PEI, MARIO. *The Story of Language.* New York: J. B. Lippincott Co., 1949.

ROBERTS, PAUL. *English Sentences.* New York: Harcourt, Brace and World, 1962.

SAPIR, EDWARD. *Language: An Introduction to the Study of Speech.* New York: Harcourt, Brace and World, 1921.

SCHLAUCH, MARGARET. *The Gift of Language.* New York: Dover Publications, 1955.

SLEDD, JAMES B. *A Short Introduction to English Grammar.* Chicago: Scott, Foresman and Co., 1959.

STURTEVANT, EDGAR H. *An Introduction to Linguistic Science.* New Haven, Conn.: Yale University Press, 1947.

TRAGER, G. L., and SMITH, HENRY LEE, JR. *An Outline of English Structure.* Washington, D.C.: American Council of Learned Societies, 1951.

VALLINS, G. H. *The Pattern of English.* New York: Oxford University Press, 1956.

WHITEHALL, HAROLD. *Structural Essentials of English.* New York: Harcourt, Brace and World, 1956.

WHORF, BENJAMIN LEE. *Language, Thought, and Reality: Selected Writings.* Cambridge, Mass.: M.I.T. Press, 1956.

BIBLIOGRAPHY OF PAPERBACKS ON LANGUAGE AND LINGUISTICS

Prepared by Kenneth G. Wilson
University of Connecticut

ALEXANDER, HENRY. *The Story of Our Language.* New York: Dolphin-Doubleday, 1962. 95¢.

ALLEN, HAROLD B. *Readings in Applied English Linguistics.* New York: Appleton-Century-Crofts, 1958. $3.75.

BABCOCK, C. MERTON. *The Ordeal of American English.* Boston: Houghton-Mifflin, 1961. $1.75.

BLACK, MAX. *The Importance of Language.* Englewood Cliffs, N.J.: Spectrum-Prentice-Hall, 1962. $1.95.

BRADDOCK, RICHARD. *Introductory Readings on the English Language.* Englewood Cliffs, N.J.: Prentice-Hall, 1962. $2.95.

BROWN, DONA, and OTHERS. *Form in Modern English.* New York: Oxford University Press, 1958. $2.90.

CASSIRER, ERNST. *Language and Myth.* New York: Dover Publications, 1946. $1.25.

CHASE, STUART. *The Tyranny of Words*. New York: Harvest-Harcourt, Brace and World, 1959. $1.95.

DEAN, LEONARD F., and WILSON, KENNETH G. *Essays on Language and Usage*. Revised edition. New York: Oxford Publications, 1963. $3.25.

GREENOUGH, JAMES B., and KITTREDGE, G. L. *Words and Their Ways in English Speech*. Boston: Beacon Press, 1962. $1.95.

HALL, ROBERT A., JR. *Linguistics and Your Language*. New York: Anchor-Doubleday & Co., 1960. $1.45.

JESPERSEN, OTTO. *Growth and Structure of the English Language*. New York: Anchor-Doubleday & Co., 1955. 95¢.

LAIRD, CHARLTON. *The Miracle of Language*. New York: Premier-Fawcett Publications, 1951. 50¢.

LAIRD, CHARLTON, and GORRELL, ROBERT M. *English as Language: Backgrounds, Development, Usage*. New York: Harcourt, Brace and World, 1961. $2.45.

MARCKWARDT, ALBERT H. *American English*. New York: Oxford University Press, 1958. $1.95.

OGDEN, C. K., and RICHARDS, I. A. *The Meaning of Meaning*. New York: Harvest-Harcourt, Brace and World, 1959. $2.25.

POTTER, SIMEON. *Language in the Modern World*. Baltimore: Pelican-Penguin, 1960. 95¢.

SAPIR, EDWARD. *Language*. New York: Harvest-Harcourt, Brace and World, 1963. $1.15.

SCHLAUCH, MARGARET. *The Gift of Language*. New York: Dover Publications, 1955. $1.85.

SLEDD, JAMES, and EBBITT, WILMA R. *Dictionaries and THAT Dictionary*. Chicago: Scott, Foresman and Co., 1962. $2.25.

STURTEVANT, E. H. *Introduction to Linguistic Science*. New Haven, Conn.: Yale University Press, 1960. $1.45.

STURTEVANT, E. H. *Linguistic Change*. Chicago: Phoenix-Chicago, 1960. $1.

THURMAN, KELLY. *Semantics*. Boston: Houghton-Mifflin, 1960. $1.75.

WEEKLEY, E. *The Romance of Words*. New York: Dover Publications, 1960. $1.25.

WHATMOUGH, JOSHUA. *Language: Modern Synthesis*. New York: St. Martin's Press, 1956. 50¢.

WILSON, KENNETH G.; HENDRICKSON, R. H.; and TAYLOR, PETER A. *Harbrace Guide to Dictionaries*. New York: Harcourt, Brace and World, 1963. $2.50.

BIBLIOGRAPHY: THEME READER PROGRAMS

BARRY, MARGARET. "The Lay Reader Program in Des Moines." *Iowa English Bulletin* 10:12-13; December 1959.

BURKE, VIRGINIA M. "A Candid Opinion on Lay Readers." *The English Journal* 50:258-64; April 1961.

———. *The Lay Reader Program: Backgrounds and Procedures*. Milwaukee: Wisconsin Council of Teachers of English (3700 North 75th Street, Milwaukee 16), 1961. 26 pp. 50¢.

DIEDERICH, PAUL B. "Readers, Aides, and Technicians." *Harvard Graduate School of Education Bulletin* 6:2-7; Spring 1961.

FORD, PAUL M. "Lay Readers in the High School Composition Program: Some Statistics." *The English Journal* 50:522-28; November 1961.

GROSE, LOIS. "Essential Conditions for Teaching Written Composition." *The English Journal* 50:246-51; April 1961. Includes a description of a theme reader plan as tested in 20 cities.

HACH, CLARENCE W. "128 Apply as Lay Readers." *Your High School* 10:3; June 1960. (Published by the Evanston Township High School.)
————. "Use of Readers for Themes Meets with Teachers' Approval." *Your High School* 11:3; February 1961.

HANDEL, HARVEY, and OTHERS. "Pupils Learn To Write in Junior High School Lay Reader Program." *The English Record* 35-44; Fall 1960. (Published by the New York State English Council, State University College, Plattsburgh, N.Y.)

KRUEGER, PAUL H. "Some Questions on the Lay Reader Program." *The English Journal* 50:529-33; November 1961.

PHILLIPS, MARY. "The Lay-Reader Program in Durham." *North Carolina English Teacher* 18:5-6; December 1960.

SAUER, EDWIN H. *Contract Correcting: The Use of Lay Readers in the High School Composition Program.* Cambridge, Mass.: Committee on Contract Correcting, Graduate School of Education, Harvard University, 1961. 59 pp.

STAFF REPORTER. "Lay Readers for Academic English Classes, Grade 12." *Staff Reporter* 14:1; October 1961. Wilmington, Delaware, Public Schools.

VAN SCHAICK, SALLY. "The Composition-Reading Machine." *The English Journal* 49:237-41; April 1960.

Appendix D:

Officials of the National Education Association, the Nine Demonstration Centers, and Directors of the Project

NEA OFFICIALS

Lois Edinger	President
Richard D. Batchelder	Vice-President
Robert H. Wyatt	Immediate Past President
Lyman V. Ginger	Treasurer
William G. Carr	Executive Secretary
Lyle W. Ashby	Deputy Executive Secretary
Lawrence G. Derthick	Assistant Executive Secretary for Educational Services

THE NINE DEMONSTRATION CENTERS OF THE NEA-DEAN LANGMUIR PROJECT ON IMPROVING ENGLISH COMPOSITION

ARDMORE, PENNSYLVANIA
Lower Merion School District

PHILIP U. KOOPMAN, Superintendent

ELWOOD PRESTWOOD, Assistant Superintendent and Director of Project

BALTIMORE, MARYLAND
Baltimore Public Schools

George Brain, Superintendent

Laurence G. Paquin, Superintendent, 1965-

Vernon S. Vavrina, Assistant Superintendent

Sidney N. Chernak, Director of Junior and Senior High Schools

Elsa Graser, Director of Project

CLEVELAND HEIGHTS, OHIO
Cleveland Heights City School District

Theos I. Anderson, Superintendent

Leonard Freyman, English and Library Coordinator and Director of Project

GREENSBORO, NORTH CAROLINA
Greensboro City Schools

P. J. Weaver, Superintendent

Sara Mims, Head of English Department and Director of Project

LAKE CHARLES, LOUISIANA
Calcasieu Parish School Board

William Dodd, Superintendent

Clint Hanchey, Assistant Superintendent

Kathleen Levingston, Director of High School English and Director of Project

LANSING, MICHIGAN
Lansing Public Schools

Forrest G. Averill, Superintendent

William R. Manning, Superintendent, 1964-

John D. Marrs, Director of Special Services and Director of Project

RICHMOND, VIRGINIA
Richmond Public Schools

H. I. Willett, Superintendent

L. D. Adams, Assistant Superintendent

Nancy Gary, Chairman of English Department and Director of Project, 1962-64

Robert T. Anderson, Director of Project, 1964-

SEATTLE, WASHINGTON
Seattle Public Schools

Ernest W. Campbell, Superintendent

Lyle Stewart, Assistant Superintendent

Helen F. Olson, Director of English Language Arts and Director of Project

WICHITA, KANSAS
Wichita Public Schools

LAWRENCE SHEPOSIER,
Superintendent

FLOYD FARMER, Assistant Superintendent

NANCY MILLETT, Director of
Project

DIRECTORS OF THE PROJECT
Arno Jewett, 1962-63
Charles E. Bish, 1963-

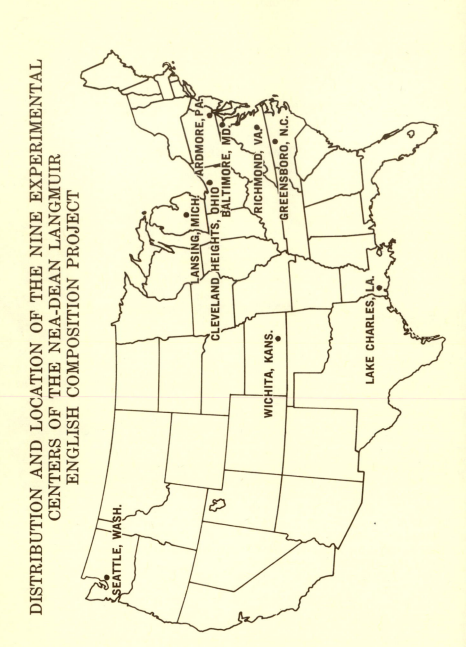

DISTRIBUTION AND LOCATION OF THE NINE EXPERIMENTAL
CENTERS OF THE NEA-DEAN LANGMUIR
ENGLISH COMPOSITION PROJECT

Appendix E:

About the Project Directors

Elwood L. Prestwood

Elwood L. Prestwood, assistant superintendent of schools for the Lower Merion School District, Ardmore, Pennsylvania, was awarded his B.A. at Columbia University, his M.A. at Lehigh University, and his Ed.D. at Columbia University. Dr. Prestwood was head of the English Department at Slatington High School in Pennsylvania for 12 years and supervising principal of Slatington Public Schools for seven years. Later he served as research associate with the Public Education Association of New York, and as lecturer with Teachers College, Columbia University; Lehigh University; the University of Pennsylvania; and Temple University. Dr. Prestwood has served on the Adolescents Commission, Association for Supervision and Curriculum Development; Department of Supervision and Curriculum, Pennsylvania State Education Association; and the Pennsylvania State Curriculum Commission. He is the coauthor of several books.

Elsa R. Graser

Elsa R. Graser received her B.A. from Goucher College, Baltimore, and her Ph.D. in Latin from Johns Hopkins University, Baltimore, in 1940. She has been a teacher in the Baltimore City Public Schools (secondary level) from 1931 to the present and, in addition, is an instructor in writing at McCoy College, Johns Hopkins University, a position she has held since 1957.

Kathleen B. Levingston

Kathleen B. Levingston was awarded her B.S. degree in 1942, her M.A. in 1958, and her Ph.D. in 1961, all from Louisiana State University. She has taught English and French in the high schools of Calcasieu and East Baton Rouge Parishes, Louisiana. Dr. Levingston is presently supervisor of English and Foreign Language Instruction, Calcasieu Parish Schools, Louisiana, and a member of several professional, honorary, and social organizations. She is the author of a number of articles on the teaching of literature and English composition.

Leonard Freyman

Leonard Freyman received his B.A. in 1939, his M.A. in 1940, and his Ph.D. in 1955, all from the Western Reserve University, Cleveland, Ohio. He studied also at Michigan State University; the Royal Academy of Dramatic Art, London, England; and Oxford University, Oxford, England. Dr. Freyman's teaching experience was obtained in the Cleveland and Cleveland Heights schools; the Department of Education, Alberta, Canada; and Fenn College, Cleveland, Ohio; and as consultant with Dale Carnegie and Associates, New York. During the year 1964 he served as lecturer at several English workshops. Dr. Freyman was a member of the Western Reserve University Board of Governors from 1957 to 1961 and since that time has been associated with a number of other organizations in the educational field.

Sara Mims

Sara Mims received her B.A. degree from Women's College, now the University of North Carolina. She majored in languages—English, Spanish, and French. Her first teaching position was at Gastonia, North Carolina, where she was head of the French Department and later of the English Department. Miss Mims was also dean of girls. From Gastonia she went to the Greensboro Public Schools as head of the English Department, and she occupies that position at the present time.

John D. Marrs

John D. Marrs received both the B.A. and M.A. degrees from Michigan State University, majoring in journalism and American literature. His professional experience includes news writing, teaching, and related public relations work on television and other media. At present he is director for information services of the Lansing Public Schools.

Robert T. Anderson

Robert T. Anderson received his Ed.D. degree from the George Peabody College for Teachers in Nashville, Tennessee. He has been a secondary school teacher and has taught in elementary and junior high schools in Montgomery, Alabama. He is a native of Alabama. Dr. Anderson came to the Richmond Public Schools in the fall of 1964 as supervisor of language arts and director of the Project on English Composition.

Nancy Gary (1962-64)

Nancy Gary received her B.A. from the College of William and Mary and her M.A. from Columbia University. She has taught in elementary, junior, and senior high schools. She was chairman of the summer workshops in Richmond which prepared guides for teaching English in grades 8 through 12, during the years 1960, 1961, and 1962, and served as chairman of the summer workshop which produced a sequential program in English composition, grades 7 through 12, in 1964. Miss Gary is at present head of the Department of English, Thomas Jefferson High School, Richmond.

Helen F. Olson

Helen F. Olson, director of the English Language Arts for the Seattle Public Schools, obtained the degrees of B.A. in education and M.A. at the University of Washington. Her graduate work was done at Columbia Teachers College, Stanford University, and the University of California. After experience as a high school teacher and department head, she served as a supervisor of English for veterans, Seattle Public Schools, during and just after World War II. She also served as instructor, lecturer, and consultant during summers at the University of Washington, Montana State University, University of Oregon, University of Utah, and Utah State Agricultural College. Miss Olson has numerous published articles to her credit and is coauthor or editor of several textbooks in the field of English.

Nancy C. Millett

Nancy C. Millett received her B.A. and M.A. degrees from the University of Rochester, New York. During the next six years she taught freshman and sophomore English at the University of Rochester and spent a year in England. While studying at the University of Illinois and the University of Wichita (Kansas), she became interested in teaching in the public schools and taught university freshmen and adult education courses. Since 1960 she has taught a variety of courses at Wichita High School East. She is a member of local, state, and national teachers organizations and of the National Council of Teachers of English.

#198 7230 A